THE COMPLETE HOME
LIGHTING
BOOK

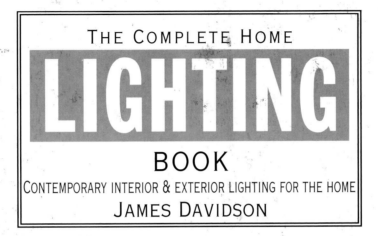

THE COMPLETE HOME
LIGHTING
BOOK
CONTEMPORARY INTERIOR & EXTERIOR LIGHTING FOR THE HOME
JAMES DAVIDSON

THE OVERLOOK PRESS
WOODSTOCK · NEW YORK

First published in the United States in 1997 by
The Overlook Press
Lewis Hollow Road
Woodstock, New York 12498

By arrangement with Cassell Publishers Ltd, London

Created by Inklink, Greenwich, London
Designed by Simon Jennings
Illustrations Robin Harris and David Day
Text edited by Albert Jackson
Assistant designer James Cross
Typeset by Amanda Allchin

Technical US advisor James Thomas Long
Lighting Design Faculty, Parsons School of Design NYC

Library of Congress Cataloging-in-Publication Data

The complete home lighting book : contemporary interior and exterior
lighting for the home/ James Davidson.
p. cm.
Includes index.
1. Dwellings–Lighting. 2. Interior decoration. 3. Exterior Lighting.
1. Title.
TK4255. D38 1997 747'.92–dc21 96-45709 CIP
ISBN: 0-87951-766-2
Printed in Spain.
First American Edition
9 8 7 6 5 4 3 2 1

DEDICATION

*To Dave and Kath Baker, without whose hospitality
this book might never have been written.*

ACKNOWLEDGEMENTS

The author would like to thank Marion and Basil Davidson,
Lionel Saph, Stephen Wynne and Clive Kay for the help they
have given me in their various ways.

PICTURE ACKNOWLEDGEMENTS

The publisher would like to thank the following for their kind permission to
reproduce the photographs in this book: Elizabeth Whiting Associates,
British Home Stores, Christopher Wray, Davey & Co., GE Lighting,
Lightbox, Oase, Optelma AG, Science Photo Library,
Stapeley Water Gardens, Stephen Wynne, Sylvania, Visual Arts Library.
Full details can be found on page 160.

CONTENTS

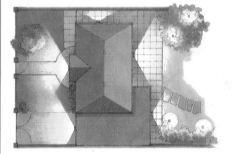

INTRODUCTION

WHEN PLANNING TO REDECORATE A ROOM, surprisingly few people consider how they are going to light it. Some may remember about north- and south-facing rooms and what effect natural light may have, but it is rare that anyone will consider light as an integral part of planning a decorative scheme, and one that should be considered at an early stage. Much thought and consideration will be given to paint finishes, wallcoverings, curtains and carpet. Some may think of upholstery. And while many people will give thought to the luminaires as objects, very few will consider the light emitted by those luminaires as an important part of the scheme or realize how fundamentally the end result will be affected by light.

It is probably true to say that, to most people, lighting means no more than the luminaire and the shade, but these are only two parts of the equation. Light is defined not simply by the quality of its presence but also that of its absence. The luminaire, a table lamp for example, will have been chosen to suit the style of a room, but it is the quality of light it gives that will help to create that style. A glance into the world of art may help to explain further.

The technique known as chiaroscuro (patterns of light and shade) has been used for centuries to instil meaning and drama into painting. Two pictures from the seventeenth century, both by Caravaggio, illustrate perfectly quite different but equally successful uses of the technique. The first, *The Crucifixion of St Peter*, makes powerful use of strong light and shade contrast to inject life, realism and drama into what is already a dramatic subject, almost forcing the viewer to share the agony of the moment. The second, *Supper at Emmaus*, uses a much gentler approach appropriate to what is a much quieter event.

From the techniques of the old masters to the complex lighting of a theatrical production, from the deliberately achieved warm glow of a good restaurant to dazzling illumination of architecture by night – the objective remains the same, to influence mood and response through well-planned use of light, shade and colour.

The aim of this book is to show how to bring this well-established range of techniques to bear in home decoration, to demystify the whole subject, to show something of what can be achieved and to give advice on how to achieve it by practical and affordable means. If you intend to redecorate completely, now is the time to plan the lighting. If not, this book shows what can be done simply by changing the position of a light or the wattage of its lamp. Starting by defining some of the more common terms, the book goes on to discuss the nature of light itself, how that light is produced, and follows with a room-by-room tour of the house and garden, with practical information and design ideas.

CHIAROSCURO
(PATTERNS OF LIGHT AND SHADE)

These two paintings by the seventeenth-century Italian artist Caravaggio demonstrate clearly the use of the contrast between light and shade known as chiaroscuro. This technique of the art world illustrates well the ideas within this book. It is fundamental to understanding the use of light that we understand its relationship to the shadow it casts, since it is that relationship which we will exploit to create the atmospheres we seek.

CHAPTER ONE

LIGHTING DEFINITIONS

THIS IS AN INTRODUCTION TO THE DEFINITIONS AND LANGUAGE USED WITHIN THIS BOOK AND WHICH RELATE TO THE SUBJECT OF LIGHTING IN OUR HOME ENVIRONMENT, BOTH INDOORS AND OUT. THIS IS AN ESSENTIAL PRELUDE TO THIS DIVERSE AND EXCITING TOPIC, ENABLING LIGHTING TO BE CONSIDERED AS AN INTEGRAL PART OF OUR ENVIRONMENT RATHER THAN SOMETHING THAT EXISTS IN ISOLATION.

DEFINITIONS

As with any area of human endeavour, lighting has spawned its own jargon, much of which is quite meaningless to the uninitiated. Since one purpose of this book is to demystify the subject, let us start by defining our terms.

THE LIGHT SOURCE

The words used to describe lighting can be very confusing. For most people, a lamp is something you plug a bulb into, which becomes a light. The professionals tend to say a luminaire is something you plug a lamp into which gives light. For the purposes of this book, I am going to use the professional terms since, once you have the hang of them, they allow for much better understanding.

BULB:

the glass envelope that contains the filament – this can be described as clear, frosted, pearl, coloured, reflective, etc.

LAMP:

the light source comprising the bulb, filament and its appropriate fitting – bayonet clip, Edison screw (screw base in the USA), etc. – this term is also used to describe fluorescent tubes.

LAMP HOLDER:

the device into which you plug the lamp.

BODY:

that which holds the lamp holder, often purely decorative.

SHADE:

that which conceals the lamp from direct view – often intended to be decorative in itself.

LUMINAIRE:

the whole thing – lamp, lamp holder, body, shade, etc.

LIGHT:

the beam or glow of light emitted by the lamp.

SPOT:

a beam of light of an angle less than 30°.

FLOOD:

a beam of light of an angle greater than 30°.

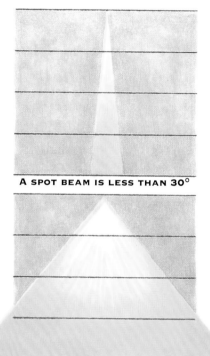

A SPOT BEAM IS LESS THAN 30°

A FLOOD BEAM IS GREATER THAN 30°

A TYPICAL LIGHT SOURCE
The lamp, the lamp holder, the body and the shade are all known collectively as a luminaire.

DEFINITIONS

THE LUMINAIRES

The names given to luminaires are generally more descriptive and readily understood, but I include the common types for easy reference.

CENTRAL PENDANT:

a luminaire suspended from an outlet, or rose, fixed to the ceiling.

LIGHTING TRACK:

a linear power socket.

DOWN-LIGHTER:

a luminaire that is designed to shine downwards only – this is known as a downlight in the USA.

RECESSED DOWN-LIGHTER:

a down-lighter mounted within the ceiling cavity.

SURFACE-MOUNTED DOWN-LIGHTER:

one mounted directly to the ceiling or a track.

DIRECTIONAL DOWN-LIGHTER:

one whose lamp holder can be moved.

WALL-MOUNTED DOWN-LIGHTER:

a wall light intended to shine downwards only.

UP-LIGHTER:

a luminaire designed to shine upwards only – known as an uplight in the USA.

WALL-MOUNTED UP-LIGHTER:

a wall light intended to shine upwards only.

SURFACE-MOUNTED UP-LIGHTER:

one mounted directly to the floor or a track.

FREE-STANDING UP-LIGHTER:

an up-lighter with a trailing lead, that does not need to be fixed in one place only.

TABLE LAMP:

a free-standing lamp holder with a short decorative body.

STANDARD LAMP:

a free-standing lamp holder with a tall decorative body.

DOWN-LIGHTING

Top: Although not designed as a down-lighter, this conventional table light has been converted into one by the use of an appropriate lamp and shade.
Bottom: In this narrow hallway, recessed down-lighters have been used to illuminate the floor and provide the practical light.

FORMS OF LIGHT

Throughout this book, I will be using terms to describe light itself which may not be familiar to all readers, and it will be useful to define these briefly here.

Precise definition of any of these terms is made difficult by the fact that context is all-important. What may be a practical light in one place may be simply decorative, and therefore only accent light, in another. Similarly, indirect light may not be intended to illuminate any particular object – just the room or space in general.

PRACTICAL OR TASK LIGHT:

light meant primarily to illuminate a task or human function.

ACCENT LIGHT:

light meant primarily to be decorative or to illuminate an object or surface.

AMBIENT LIGHT:

the quality and quantity of light within a given space, created by the sum of the above.

DIRECT LIGHT:

light which shines directly onto an object or surface.

INDIRECT LIGHT:

light which is reflected onto an object or surface.

NATURAL LIGHT:

light which exists in nature, most commonly sunlight.

SHADOW (OR SHADE):

is created by the presence of light.

DARKNESS:

can be defined as the absence of light.

ACCENT LIGHT
This small wall light provides an accent in what might otherwise be a dark corner of the room.

15

CHAPTER TWO

LIGHTING GENERAL PRINCIPLES

THIS BOOK IS ALL ABOUT LIGHTING OUR HOMES, BOTH INSIDE THE HOUSE AND OUTSIDE IN THE GARDEN. THIS IS NOT TO SAY THAT WE SHOULD CONSIDER LIGHTING IN ISOLATION: GOOD DOMESTIC LIGHTING, LIKE GOOD LIGHTING ANYWHERE, IS NOT JUST THE BUSINESS OF ILLUMINATION, BUT IS INTEGRAL TO THE WAY WE DECORATE AND FURNISH OUR HOMES. OF ALL ASPECTS OF DOMESTIC DESIGN, LIGHTING HAS THE MOST PROFOUND EFFECT ON THE ATMOSPHERE OF OUR HOMES AND CONSEQUENTLY TO THE WAY WE FEEL ABOUT OURSELVES AND THE WAY WE ARE PERCEIVED BY OUR VISITORS.

THEORY & PRACTICE

LIGHTING DESIGN, LIKE MOST PRACTICAL ACTIVITIES, FALLS INTO
TWO PARTS — THE THEORY AND THE PRACTICE. THE NATURE OF
LIGHT AND HOW IT AFFECTS OUR MOODS AND RESPONSES IS THE
THEORY. THE LUMINAIRES AND LAMPS THEMSELVES, AND WHERE TO
USE THEM, CONSTITUTE THE PRACTICE.

DESIGNING FOR ATMOSPHERE
*Opposite: Gloomy weather cannot
dispel the golden glow in this garden
sitting room. Natural materials,
indoor planting and the colour of the
lampshades all conspire to provide
warmth and comfort.*

THE NATURE OF LIGHT

Professional interior designers who specialize in commercial
interiors are aware of these issues, particularly those that relate
to the creation of mood, but an understanding of how one can
use light as a feature of interior design is essential for anyone
who is interested in their environment and seeks to make the
best of it. In truth, however, most people are no more than the
unwitting targets of lighting design.

This is not to suggest that there is anything sinister about it,
but rather to show that the quality of light we experience has a
profound (and acknowledged) effect on us, and that light can be
used to induce specific moods in an observer. I hope to make
clear what the essential qualities of light are and how we can
exploit them to enhance our lives and make our houses into the
homes we dream about.

HUMAN TARGETS

When I say targets, I mean only that we are the ultimate users of
designed lighting, whether or not we are aware of it. Light is
used in many different places for many different purposes. A
large proportion of the artificial light around us is practical;
that is to say, it is intended to provide illumination so that
certain tasks or functions can be performed efficiently and
safely. These include getting on or off a train, entering or
leaving a building, or finding one's way after dark. All practical
light has been designed to some extent, but there are situations
where the light is deliberately organized to induce a specific
mood or frame of mind.

LIGHT IN RETAIL
*This bookshop in London's
Westminster Abbey uses delicate
low-voltage projectors to illuminate
the books and strong up-lighters to
provide a sense of grandeur.*

SPECIFIC REQUIREMENTS

PERHAPS THE TWO MOST COMMON USERS OF DESIGNED LIGHTING ARE THE LEISURE AND RETAIL SECTORS. WHILST SMALLER BUSINESSES MAY PROVIDE THE CORRECT LIGHTING BY INSTINCT, MANY HIGH-STREET RETAILERS, PARTICULARLY THE BIG CHAINS AND FRANCHISES, HAVE VERY SPECIFIC LIGHTING REQUIREMENTS, ALL OF WHICH ARE INTENDED TO INDUCE AND ENABLE YOU TO BUY THEIR GOODS. CORRECT LIGHTING CAN BE A VERY SIGNIFICANT PART OF THE SALES STRATEGY.

SPECIFIC MOODS   A supermarket, for example, may use just the right colour-temperature fluorescent tubes to enhance the colours printed on the packaging, and will avoid any lighting which might dazzle. They will tend to provide good ambient light with 'special-offer' highlights, to enable customers to see everything clearly and to encourage them to buy certain items. In pubs, clubs and restaurants, the intention is to make you relax and feel at ease, to induce a feeling of quiet well-being – overall, the lighting will be quite subdued, but locally, bright enough to see the menu and your fellow diners – to encourage you to stay and thus spend more money! The quality of the light is no less important than the quality of the food and service, and an ill-lit restaurant can actually deter customers.

Banks, corporate headquarters and exclusive hotels might wish to instil a measure of reverence or calm in their visitors, to create an atmosphere of quiet sophistication and command respect. A subtle, elegant lighting scheme will go a long way towards achieving this, and many such companies will have had luminaires designed and manufactured as a part of their corporate identity.

ELEGANTLY PRACTICAL
This low-voltage track system provides a good practical light to the stairwell and a lot of visual interest and sparkle to the space as a whole.

DRAMATIC NIGHTSCAPE
Left: Powerful up-light combined with subtly placed down-lighting for the plants prevents this inspiring view of the city at sunset from becoming too vertiginous and yet allows it to be seen clearly.

A LIGHT TO DINE BY
By using projectors as down-lighters, this restaurant provides good light to dine by without overwhelming the diners. The low-voltage lamps bring out the glassware particularly well.

EXCEPTIONS TO THE RULE

There are exceptions, of course. The business of a fast-food restaurant is bulk sales, and it relies on a high turnover of meals to achieve its target. In these circumstances a restaurant may be lit deliberately to prevent the customers from relaxing, with the intention that they will leave sooner and allow others to use their table.

Nightclubs, and dance clubs in particular, will wish to achieve the opposite from the pub or restaurant, actively seeking to excite and stimulate, not necessarily with a high level of bright light but with strong, focused and often animated lighting, on and off the dance floor. Nightclubs are places of entertainment – places where the customer is encouraged to forget the world outside, and the lighting will be intended to create mystery, excitement and even fantasy.

DOMESTIC APPLICATIONS

Although few domestic lighting budgets will stretch to custom-made luminaires, all and any of the ideas and tricks that are regularly used in commerce can be adapted for the home, but it is important to know first what it is we are dealing with, particularly since the subject of lighting can be very confusing.

LIGHTING DESIGN

LIGHTING FOR THE JOB
Opposite: In this space, busy with shape and pattern, the light is used to emphasize the forms and yet provides good practical illumination where it is needed.

IN SEEKING TO UNDERSTAND THE BUSINESS OF LIGHTING AS AN INTEGRAL PART OF INTERIOR DESIGN, IT HELPS TO STOP THINKING OF 'LIGHTS' AS THINGS BOUGHT FROM A SHOP AND START TO THINK ABOUT 'LIGHT' AS SOMETHING TO BE PLAYED WITH. LIGHT IS, AFTER ALL, ONLY A BEAM OF VARYING WIDTH AND INTENSITY COMING FROM A SPECIFIC PLACE, WHETHER THAT BE THE SUN OR A CANDLE, AND IT IS AVAILABLE IN AN ALMOST INFINITE VARIETY OF TONE, COLOUR AND STRENGTH. WHEN WE TALK OF 'LIGHTING A ROOM', WE THINK WE MEAN THE INSTALLATION OF VARIOUS NUMBERS AND TYPES OF LIGHT FITTING (OR LUMINAIRE). BUT WHAT WE ACTUALLY MEAN IS THE QUALITY OF THE LIGHT EMITTED FROM THOSE LUMINAIRES, AND, INSEPARABLE FROM THE LIGHT, THE SHADOWS FORMED BY IT.

LIGHT SOURCES

All sources of light have their own distinct qualities of tone and colour, and what is appropriate for any given project depends on the space being illuminated and the purpose for which that space will be used. For example, a sitting room will require a quite different style of lighting from a bathroom. Just as natural forms of light have unique qualities, so do artificial ones, and the choice will be dictated by the intent.

MODELLING WITH LIGHT
Light from the room throws shadow into the alcove, establishing the form of the chimney breast. The up-lighter prevents the plants from becoming dominant by adding interest to the alcove itself and, because it is placed high on the wall, does not interfere with the sense of depth.

QUALITY OR QUANTITY

One thing is certain, more light is not the same as good light. There are places within the home where the more light you can provide the better, but they will be the exceptions rather than the rule. Generally, simply flooding a space with light does not take into account, and will not satisfy, any of the requirements for mood and atmosphere. Irrespective of how many light sources there are in a room, it is the quality of the light emitted that counts.

CONTRAST

Light creates shadows, which produce depth, define form and allow for highlights and focal points. Mood and atmosphere are achieved by the contrast and balance between light and shadow; it is this balance which makes a room feel cosy and welcoming or, conversely, cold and uncomfortable. Naturally this depends

SHADOW AS MOOD
Above left: In this example, shadow is used to create mood rather than form. The whole group is interesting, particularly the luminaire, but the sense of intimacy, almost of secrecy, is achieved by using a heavy, dark shade that produces a strong down-light.

WELCOMING LIGHT
Above right: A similar effect is sought in this quiet corner. The fundamental difference is that the warm, mid-tone colour of this shade invites us in rather than excludes us. It also lifts a space that might otherwise be dominated by the picture group by projecting the light through the foliage of a plant.

LIGHT FROM MANY SOURCES
Right: A classic example of many light sources used in harmony. The standard, table and pendant luminaires are backed up by natural light from the window, and borrowed light from the kitchen.

24

to some extent on the local climate and individual taste – in a hot climate, a cool, shady room would be most welcome, during the day at least.

Contrary to popular belief, it is shadow, not light, that gives form to objects. A three-dimensional object or space can very easily become flattened out and lose its shape under incorrect lighting. Too much light is no better than too little – it is possible to drown something with a floodlight. Conversely, it is possible to enhance or alter the shape of something by lighting it in certain ways.

As we have seen, the balance of light and shade can instil a specific frame of mind or feeling. In terms of design, although the luminaires may be integral to the style of the interior, they are not the light. The luminaire and its shade, if any, will have an effect on the quality and quantity of the light in a room, but it is the combination of the tone, intensity and focus of the 'lamp' which makes the 'light'.

LIGHT FROM A SINGLE SOURCE
One well-placed light source, in this case a spotlight, illuminates this hallway and produces a dramatic scene framed by the door. The angle of the projector is such that it creates striking contrast and good, solid modelling. But this is lighting for accent; to sit in the chair would be most uncomfortable.

LIGHT AS CONTROL

The minimalism of the furnishing in this room is reflected in the lighting. Here it is the light rather than the shadow which is doing the work – the natural light from the window illuminates the space during the day, with the only artificial lighting being the picture lights – but all is very diffuse and free from shadow. The effect encourages a contemplative mood but stimulates the intellect by almost obliging one to concentrate on the pictures.

STRONG ACCENTS

In contrast, this high-tech lighting gantry makes no pretence to subtlety. Lighting of this sort commands attention, and one is left in no doubt where to look. It is this sort of strong accent light that is used in art galleries, museums and retail outlets to focus the viewer onto specific subjects.

THE QUALITIES OF LIGHT

IN SEEKING TO UNDERSTAND THE QUALITIES OF LIGHT, IT IS IMPORTANT TO BEAR IN MIND THAT WHAT IS TRUE IN NATURE IS TRUE IN ARTIFICE. WHETHER CONSCIOUSLY OR SUBCONSCIOUSLY, WE ALL REGISTER THE MOODS AND ATMOSPHERES EXPERIENCED IN NATURAL LIGHT, AND IT IS THESE THAT ARE THE SOURCE OF INSPIRATION FOR THE LIGHTING DESIGNER. IT IS BY ANALYZING AND UNDERSTANDING THE QUALITIES OF NATURAL LIGHT THAT WE ARE ABLE TO REALIZE OUR IDEAS.

TONE, INTENSITY & FOCUS

All sources of light have their own particular qualities, some which are the result of the light source itself and some the result of external influences, such as the weather and the landscape. The light from the sun, for example, is constantly changing, depending on the time of day, the time of year, the weather, the latitude at which it is observed, and so on. If one is conscious of the tone of the light around one, it is quite possible to analyze the causes and influences which create that particular effect, and to reproduce it by artificial means. This is no less true for the garden than for the house, and the result will be an effective combination of natural and artificial light.

The quality of any light, whether natural or artificial, can be defined in three, quite simple ways: tone, intensity and focus.

TONE

The tone of a light is defined by its colour temperature. The temperature of light is synonymous with its colour, in that they are both a product of a specific wavelength. The primary colours of natural light make up the spectrum of colours that can be seen when light is split by a prism; at one end of the scale is ultraviolet – the blue end – and at the other is infrared – the red end of the visible spectrum. The light we see and see by is a mixture of all these and is described as white, but all light sources have their own colour; that is, they emit a distinct wavelength pattern, depending on what they are designed to do.

TONE, INTENSITY & FOCUS
The quality of light is determined by its tone, intensity and focus. The dark, heavy furniture in the picture opposite is in strong contrast to the light walls. This contrast is softened by the use of mid-tone lamps in high-level up-lighters and the sculptural use of the glass wall panel, both of which produce distinct pools of light and shade. The bright, cool foreground in the room above is a result of soft pastel colours in the décor and furnishings, combined with diffuse light from the cold-white lamps in the luminaires.

COLOUR TEMPERATURE
The qualities of a space or an object can be emphasized by using the right lamp for the situation. In the foreground, the hard, shiny objects and the strong colours of the lilies are brought out by the cold-white lamp in the luminaire. In contrast, the warm tones of the walls and floor are reflected in the wall and table luminaires in the background, both fitted with mid-tone lamps.

COLOUR TEMPERATURE
Most domestic lamps are similar in colour temperature. Generally, a tungsten-filament lamp tends to be yellow/warm, and a tungsten-halogen one, blue/cool. In reproducing natural effects, however, we can introduce secondary colour through pigment by using filters or adding colour to the bulb, and we are able to alter the balance of the light to suit the atmosphere we are trying to achieve. Do not confuse light with pigment, as they exhibit colour by quite different means. With pigment, it is possible to have cold yellow or warm blue, for example, and this adds a great deal to the possibilities.

FOCUSED LIGHT
None of the lights in this pool room are very intense, but they are all highly focused. The room as a whole is not illuminated; each luminaire is constrained to throw light that draws our attention to distinct areas, and it is the combination of them all which creates the ambient light in the room.

INTENSITY
The brightness of the light is fundamental to the quality of the atmosphere in a room. That is not to preclude the use of very bright lights, but if you are going to use them, they must be carefully controlled. Generally, a number of dim lamps will create a more interesting atmosphere than a single bright lamp, even if they add up to the same amount of light.

FOCUS
Directness of light is the result of outside influences on the light emitted from a lamp. For example, the 'bulb' or envelope containing the filament of the standard 'pearl' lamp is frosted and throws a diffuse light all around, producing a bland, featureless light. In contrast, a combination of a parabolic reflector and a crown-silvered lamp is designed to throw a very tightly focused beam, producing a dramatic light capable of giving life and shape to a room. There are many lamps and luminaires designed specifically to produce a controlled width of beam.

NATURAL EFFECTS

The atmosphere we experience in the outside world is a combination of the tone and the contrast produced by the conditions. We can begin to study those natural conditions by analyzing the tone, intensity and focus.

The quality of sunlight at noon in the Sahara desert is harsh and bright, with intense shadows. By contrast, in a deciduous wood on a wet day in the northern hemisphere, the light is muted and soft, with very little obvious shadow, the whole effect being diffuse and vague. So how do we describe these in analytic terms?

In nature a 'nice sunny day', for example, could be defined as: warm, bright, direct. A 'soft' day in Scotland might be: cool, bright, diffuse. When we are outside, our mood may be strongly influenced by these conditions, and we tend to feel a certain way about a place or scene, depending on the quality of the light. In seeking to reproduce those feelings, the same terms should apply to artificial light; they will be the key to successful lighting in your home.

LIGHT AS COLOUR

The search for an understanding of the relationship between light and mood was of primary importance to the Impressionist school of painters at the turn of the century. They sought to represent light with pigment, capturing atmosphere through colour rather than recording a scene or event purely with an image. Studying their work can teach us a lot about the colour of light and its effect on mood.

Remember that the décor within a room, the colour of its walls and so on, will have a strong impact on its mood. Light should not be considered in isolation, but as part of an overall decorative scheme. What is happening outside is also a factor and is one which you can exploit, but inside it is less to do with weather and more to do with lamp types, wattages and so on, which we will discuss next.

NATURAL LIGHT
Above: Here natural light is the main source, the central luminaire hardly contributing anything during the day. The effect is cool and soft, with an almost 'underwater' feel about it, and on a hot day such a room would be very appealing.

LIGHT AS COLOUR
The lamp in the wall-mounted luminaire is, in itself, cold and white, but because it is used to illuminate warm beige walls and ceiling, turning them yellow, the overall effect is warm and bright.

31

HOW LIGHT IS PRODUCED

ALL ARTIFICIAL LIGHT COMES FROM A LAMP OF SOME SORT, INDEED, THE DICTIONARY DEFINITION OF A LAMP IS ANY DEVICE USED TO PRODUCE ARTIFICIAL LIGHT. IN DOMESTIC LAMPS, THERE ARE THREE WAYS OF PRODUCING THAT LIGHT.

LIGHT FOR THE HOME

Put very simply, one way is incandescence – something glowing white hot. Another is fluorescence – something absorbing invisible radiation and emitting visible radiation, and the other is a flame – burning something flammable, such as oil or wax. These are not the only ways of producing light, but they are the ones used in the home.

INCANDESCENCE

This is the most common means of producing domestic light, and is the one we all think of when we say 'light bulb'. The incandescent lamp falls into two categories, which, for the sake of simplicity I will call tungsten filament and tungsten halogen.

TUNGSTEN-FILAMENT

The earliest practical 'electric light bulb' was invented by Thomas Edison in 1879. This was a carbon filament enclosed in a bulb containing a vacuum. Very simply, an electric current passing through the filament caused it to become hot and give off light. In 1907, tungsten replaced carbon for the filament because its very high melting point allowed it to glow more brightly, and in 1913, inert gases, such as argon and nitrogen, replaced the vacuum, giving the filament a longer life; today lamps of this type can be expected to last an average of 1000 hours. All lamps are given a Rated Average Life or RAL, which is the number of hours that 50% of lamps of any given type survive being left on continuously. These lamps are still the mainstay of domestic lighting, and their variations and uses are discussed on page 44. Tungsten-filament lamps tend towards the yellow/warm end of the spectrum.

LAMPS IN USE

Opposite: While all the lamps are incandescent, each of the paintings in this room is lit by the type of lamp best suited to bring out its colour. On the left, the warm reds and yellows are enhanced by a tungsten-filament lamp, while the painting on the right is lit with tungsten-halogen.

THOMAS EDISON
Though not alone in his experiments with light, in 1879 Edison produced the first practical lamp, very similar to the one illustrated below.

33

TUNGSTEN-HALOGEN

This is a relatively new type of incandescent lamp, and one that only recently has become a regular feature of domestic lighting, having been introduced from the theatre via the world of commercial-display lighting. They are made using fused-quartz glass filled with halogen and argon which achieves a high light output for relatively little energy. They are very compact compared with conventional lamps, and have a rated average life (RAL) of up to 5000 hours. Though usually in the form of small bulbs, they are also available as short tubes called 'linear halogen' lamps. Which of these you choose depends on the luminaire, the type of beam and the amount of light required.

Perhaps the most common example of these lamps in use has been traffic lights, but for interior design, the halogen lamp is used most often as a projector, because it produces a very intense, white light. When combined with a dichroic reflector, the light can be directed into a very tightly controlled beam.

One significant advantage of tungsten-halogen lamps is that they can run off much reduced voltage, usually as little as 12V. This allows very much greater flexibility for the designers of luminaires, track systems and so on, and it makes them much cheaper to run. Tungsten-halogen lamps tend towards the blue/cool end of the spectrum.

TUNGSTEN-HALOGEN
With the exception of the table lamp in the bookcase, all the artificial lighting in this room is from tungsten-halogen lamps. The down-lighters produce a good general light and their thick acrylic diffusers create a lot of sparkle with little shadow. The accent comes largely from the shadows cast by the standard up-lighter and natural daylight from the windows.

THE ESSENCE OF FLUORESCENCE
A showroom is always awkward to light since the contents will be continuously moved about. This is an ideal place for a good wash of light overall and the near daylight achieved by the lamps in this show room enables the cars to be seen at their best.

FLUORESCENCE   Fluorescent light is produced by making a phosphor coating on the inside of a tube fluoresce, or glow, by ultraviolet radiation from mercury vapour. This glow occurs at a low temperature and thus uses little energy. As a result, the RAL is up to 20,000 hours, and the running cost is very low. A 40W fluorescent tube will produce as much light as a 150W incandescent lamp.

Fluorescent light was first introduced in 1938, and was seen by many as a replacement for the 'old-fashioned' filament lamp. This is certainly true in the office and factory, and the fluorescent tube still reigns supreme in many a domestic kitchen. Unfortunately for design purposes, the light emitted, though very bright, is extremely diffuse, and tends to eliminate all shadow. Since the achievement of atmospheric light depends on shadow, eliminating it has a detrimental effect on what we are seeking to achieve and, consequently, the fluorescent tube has strictly limited appeal for domestic interior lighting. They are ideal for workshops and garages, where quantity of light is paramount and shadows are to be avoided, but fluorescent tubes should be used with care anywhere else.

The new compact fluorescent lamps are far more suitable. The development of these lamps has created new opportunities for fluorescent lighting, and it now has a very definite and increasingly useful place throughout the home, one singular advantage being that fluorescent lights burn very coolly. As a result, they can be used in places where tungsten-filament or halogen lamps would be impossible.

Whatever the situation, it is worth giving some consideration to the choice of light source available and to think of the differences each type might make on the atmosphere you are trying to achieve. Each can satisfy different needs, and has its pros and cons.

TRADITIONAL & PERIOD LIGHTING

APART FROM THE ACCEPTED 'NORMAL' LIGHT SOURCES, THERE ARE OF COURSE THE ONES WHICH ELECTRIC LIGHTING HAS TENDED TO SUPERSEDE. THESE MAKE UP THE THIRD MEANS OF PRODUCING ARTIFICIAL LIGHT MENTIONED EARLIER. THOUGH IT MAY SEEM PERVERSE TO INCLUDE THEM, THIS BOOK IS ABOUT LIGHT, NOT ELECTRICITY, AND OLDER FORMS OF LIGHTING ARE STILL VALID.

CANDLE MAKING IN THE NINETEENTH CENTURY

OLDER METHODS

It is my belief that we have had electric lighting around for long enough for it to have lost its novelty value, and it can be fun to take advantage of the more subtle light created by 'old-fashioned' methods.

Strictly speaking, the oil lamp and the candle are the same thing. They are both formed of a porous wick soaked in a flammable grease and with a reservoir of fuel. The two important differences are that one is liquid and one is solid, and one is controllable and the other is not. I don't know, and I am not aware that archaeology can tell us, which of these is the older technology, but we do know a good deal about how our forebears went about defeating the darkness.

OIL LAMPS

The oil lamp consists of a wick soaked in a bath of liquid fuel, amongst the earliest known being in use in Greece during the fourth century BC. The amount of wick exposed to the air, and therefore burning, determines the light output of the lamp – the more wick exposed the greater the amount of flame and, unfortunately, the greater the amount of smoke. The fuel would have been fish oil, and later whale oil, or oil extracted from plants such as olives or peanuts. To some extent, at least, the one you chose might have depended on your sense of smell. Mixing a perfume into the oil would have made some difference, but essentially these oils would not have been very well refined and would have produced a good deal of smoke and stench.

THE GLORY OF THE CANDLE
Opposite: A whole group of assorted candles and their holders, illustrating just how alluring older forms of lighting can be.

OIL LAMP
This cut-away illustration shows clearly the principle of the wick-in-a-bath technique still in use in the nineteenth century, many hundreds of years after its invention.

A SUBTLER WAY WITH ELECTRICITY

There will always be situations where the demand for traditional lighting cannot be met – perhaps for reasons of safety – and in such circumstances, converted traditional luminaires and concealed lighting can solve the problem. In the picture to left, the atmosphere of this mediaeval room would be destroyed by anachronistic forms of lighting, and concealed down-light has been used to good effect. Few rooms are exclusively of one period, and while a traditional light source such as the candelabra pictured above may not be contemporary with the ceiling, it is not as obtrusive as a modern luminaire. In this case it has been converted to electricity in order to preserve the paintwork.

THE WICK-IN-A-BATH The earliest form of lamp is simply a wick floating in an open bath of oil. This would have been unshaded, and would have produced no more light than a candle with a similar-sized wick. The advantage was likely to have been simplicity; once you had a container – the lamp – the wick and the oil were easily replaced as required. Lamps of this type are still available today, particularly with the rise of interest in scented oils, and they can be fun to have around.

THE ENCLOSED OIL LAMP The oil lamp we are familiar with is quite late in design, by which time the fuels would have been much more thoroughly refined, and nowadays most oil lamps burn paraffin or kerosene. The modern oil lamp combines the wick-and-bath technique with control, and often has more than one wick. The wick is flat, giving a larger flame, and the amount of wick exposed to burn is controlled by a screw; the more wick the higher the light output. The flame is contained within a glass chimney, which enables it to burn steadily and more brightly, and to make less smoke. The quality of the light from an oil lamp can be varied by the addition of a shade. A white opalescent shade will produce a cool diffuse light, for example, which is surprisingly good for practical needs. There are many styles of shade available for oil lamps, but they are mostly variations of the coloured-glass globe, and while a coloured shade will not give as much light, it can contribute greatly to the atmosphere of a room.

CANDLES A candle is one or more wicks encased in solid flammable grease. Today this will be either paraffin wax or beeswax, but traditionally, candles were also made from tallow – usually the refined hard fat of animals. Although you will have extreme difficulty obtaining a tallow candle today, there is an almost infinite variety of both practical and decorative candles on sale in specialist shops. Keeping a few candles in the house is a very sensible precaution against power failures as well as an excellent means of providing a soft, warm and welcoming atmosphere.

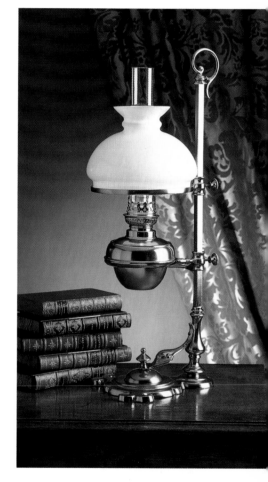

THE ENCLOSED OIL LAMP
Whether still burning oil, or converted to electricity, the range of oil lamps is as prodigious as conventional luminaires. There are table lamps, wall brackets and pendants, with almost as many varieties of shade to go with them.

DIPPED OR CAST

In the past, most candles were made by dipping a wick into a pot of hot wax. Called 'dips', they were usually made in pairs by dipping both ends in the wax at the same time. Repeated dipping would build up layer after layer of wax and produce candles of the required thickness. Candles can be produced in bulk by pouring melted wax into a mould that has a wick or wicks pre-threaded into it; more elaborate candles can be manufactured in this way.

Today there is an extensive range of moulds and other equipment available for casting candles, and a whole craft industry has grown up over recent years. Should you wish to make your own candles, whether by dipping or by casting, many beautiful and highly complex variations on the candle are possible, limited only by your ingenuity.

RUSHLIGHTS

The poorest form of candle, the rushlight was simply the soft pith of a rush dipped in tallow. So small and feeble was the glimmer given by the rushlight that it became synonymous with a lack of information or intelligence. That their use was widespread, however, is shown by the number of specially made rushlight holders that can be found amongst museum collections right across Europe and in the areas of early European settlement in America.

BEESWAX CANDLES

By contrast, the best candles were made from beeswax. These were expensive, and only the nobility and the clergy would use them regularly. Despite its relatively high cost even today, beeswax is very popular for making candles. Its colour is pleasant, but it is particularly the smell that makes beeswax so attractive – it gives off a warm aroma of honey, redolent of the balmy days of summer.

CLASSIC REPRODUCTIONS
A modern electric chandelier with lamps in the shape of candles combines the brilliance of electric illumination while retaining most of its period feel. Luminaires of this sort are often used to provide a sense of past elegance and glory.

CHANDELIERS

With the demand from the wealthy for more and more light, multiple candle holders reached almost fantastic proportions. In their heyday, chandeliers were huge collections of candles, usually suspended from the ceiling, with some large rooms being lit by perhaps thousands of candles. The holders were often adorned with cut glass to reflect the light and produce 'sparkle', and when combined with mirrored walls, these great 'crystal chandeliers' must have been an awe-inspiring sight. Modern 'chandeliers' are pale shadows of these former glories, but in the right setting, they can still provide a good all-round light. They are inclined to dominate, however, and they are at their best when combined with a dimmer so that you can vary the atmosphere as you wish for any given occasion.

GAS & MANTLE LAMPS

Gaslight was the light of the Industrial Revolution, the light of the nineteenth century. Of course, it was still around until quite recently, but although many people use gas for cooking and heating, nowadays gaslight is generally only possible in the form of the pressure lamp. Originally the gas simply burned from a nozzle, giving a relatively poor light, and it was not until the invention of the incandescent mantle that gaslight became really practical. The light produced is very bright and, although it is possible to control the level to some extent, and shades are available, for most people today, gaslight is very much emergency lighting, and as a light source it does not have much of a place in interior lighting.

IF YOU GO INTO THE LIGHTING SECTION OF ANY HARDWARE OR GENERAL STORE, YOU WILL BE MET INEVITABLY WITH AN ARRAY OF DIFFERENT LAMPS, EACH WITH A DIFFERENT FEATURE OFTEN REFERRED TO BY INITIALS, OR BY SOME WORD KNOWN ONLY TO THE SPECIALIST. THERE WILL ALSO BE SWITCHES, PLUGS, SOCKETS AND SO ON, AND I WILL DISCUSS SUCH OF THOSE AS ARE RELEVANT TO LIGHTING, AS OPPOSED TO POWER. THIS SECTION COVERS THE TECHNICAL ASPECTS OF LIGHT AND LIGHTING, AND EXPLAINS THE DIFFERENCES BETWEEN ONE SORT OF LAMP AND ANOTHER.

TYPES OF LAMP
HOW THE LIGHT IS PRODUCED

TUNGSTEN-FILAMENT

BY EXPLAINING THE TECHNICAL TERMS, I HOPE TO REDUCE THE BEWILDERMENT FELT ABOUT LIGHTING BY SO MANY PEOPLE. IT MAY BE HELPFUL HERE TO RECAP BRIEFLY ON THE TWO MAIN WAYS BY WHICH DOMESTIC LIGHT IS COMMONLY PRODUCED, INCANDESCENCE AND FLUORESCENCE.

INCANDESCENCE   This is when something glows white-hot.
Incandescent lamps for the domestic market fall into two categories: tungsten-filament and tungsten-halogen.

TUNGSTEN-HALOGEN

TUNGSTEN-FILAMENT   This is a very fine wire made from tungsten, enclosed in a glass bulb containing a mixture of argon and nitrogen. An electric current passing through the filament causes it to become white-hot and give off light.

TUNGSTEN-HALOGEN   Similar to tungsten-filament lamps, the main differences are that these are made from fused-quartz glass, filled with halogen and argon; they achieve greater light output for less energy, and can be very compact.

FLUORESCENCE   This is when something absorbs invisible radiation and emits visible radiation. A phosphor coating on the inside of a tube or bulb is made to fluoresce, or glow, by ultraviolet radiation from mercury vapour. This glow occurs at a low temperature and thus uses little energy. There is an ever-growing range of halogen and compact fluorescent lamps available, and many of the traditional filament lamps are becoming effectively obsolete as they are replaced by the more economic and longer-lasting halogen and fluorescent alternatives.

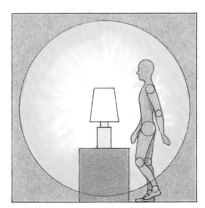

ALL-ROUND GLOW

ALL-ROUND GLOW & PROJECTORS   Broadly speaking, lamps fall into two categories, independent of the cap or filament type: those that produce an all-round glow, and those that project a beam. The former can be turned into a projector by adding a reflector to concentrate the light into a beam, but the nature of the lamp itself does not change.

PROJECTION

THE CAP
HOW THE LAMP PLUGS INTO THE LUMINAIRE

ONE COMMON PROBLEM IS RECOGNIZING THE DIFFERENT MEANS BY WHICH A LAMP PLUGS INTO THE LUMINAIRE, THAT IS, THE CAP. FOR DOMESTIC PURPOSES, LAMP CAPS FALL USUALLY INTO THREE BASIC CATEGORIES, AND WHEN BUYING A LUMINAIRE IT IS IMPORTANT THAT YOU ALSO CHOOSE THE TYPE OF LAMP THAT WILL FIT.

BASIC CAP TYPES

The three basic types of cap for domestic use are:

- Bayonet cap (BC)
- Edison screw (ES)
- Their small versions (SBC and SES)

TUNGSTEN-HALOGEN TYPE CAPS

However, with the introduction of tungsten-halogen lamps, two more cap types have been developed and are now to be found on the domestic market:

- Double pin
- Twist and lock (TAL)

All incandescent lamps and some modern compact fluorescent lamps will be fitted with one of these types of cap.

FLUORESCENT-LAMP CAPS

COMPACT FLUORESCENTS
These now have common cap types.

Fluorescent lamps have always had their own forms of cap and, since they were not interchangeable with other lamps, this has never been a problem; provided one checks the old lamp, finding the correct replacement should be straightforward. Now that consumers are more concerned with energy conservation, there is a growing demand for compact fluorescents specifically intended to replace conventional lamps, and manufacturers have started to fit the common cap types to accommodate the market. This is a period of change and there are still a number of fluorescent lamps that will only fit custom-made luminaires, but manufacturers are making strenuous efforts to supply adapters and other means to facilitate the change.

BAYONET CAP (BC)

EDISON SCREW (ES)

DOUBLE PIN

TWIST AND LOCK (TAL)

ALL-ROUND GLOW

CLEAR GLASS

THE STANDARD PEARL AND CLEAR LAMPS – KNOWN AS GENERAL LIGHTING SERVICE OR GLS LAMPS – ARE THE MOST COMMON OF THE ALL-ROUND-GLOW TYPE. THESE ARE THE LAMPS WE ARE ALL FAMILIAR WITH. WHETHER BC OR ES, THESE ARE THE LAMPS THAT FIT INTO MOST OF OUR DOMESTIC LUMINAIRES.

FROSTED GLASS

SHAPE & TYPE OF GLASS

The majority of all-round-glow lamps will be of standard shape, the traditional light bulb and its variants. There are some odd shapes such as globe lamps and candle lamps, but their shape does not affect the amount or quality of light they produce. What does affect the quality and quantity of light are the type of lamp employed and any treatment applied to the glass. All these lamps will have bulbs made either of clear or frosted glass which may also be coloured.

CLEAR GLASS

Clear-glass lamps throw a strong, sharp light that produces well-defined shadows. These lamps are not used often for general-purpose lighting because the intensity of the shadow they cast gives the impression that they emit relatively low light levels. Much more common are the various frosted or diffused lamps.

FROSTED GLASS

Frosted-glass, or pearl, lamps produce a diffuse, soft light. Because diffusion softens the shadows as well as the light, it creates the illusion of more light per watt output, and the pearl lamp is now the most common type in domestic use.

VARIATIONS

In response to the increasing public awareness of design, manufacturers are producing some interesting and useful variations on the conventional lamps, which are now commonly available. Many luminaires are designed specifically to make use of these variations, allowing us to think differently about the luminaires themselves.

THE ALL-ROUND-GLOW EFFECT

CLEAR AND FROSTED HALOGEN

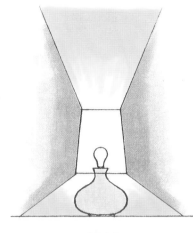

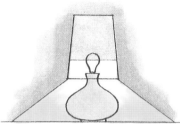

ONE LUMINAIRE – TWO JOBS

Changing the lamp can convert a table light into a down-lighter. When fitted with a regular lamp, a table light gives an all-round glow with light spilling up and down. A crown-silvered lamp will throw most of the illumination downwards, creating a more intimate light.

CROWN-SILVERED

SOFT-TONE LAMPS

As an alternative to the white pearl lamp, soft-tone lamps come in a range of subtle colours, from peach to green. These are very useful for enhancing the theme colour of a decorative scheme, and they produce a pleasant, quiet light. Because they come in all cap sizes, bulb sizes and shapes, soft-tone lamps are particularly useful for taking the hard edge off lighting, in whatever circumstances.

CROWN-SILVERED LAMPS

These are intended to be used in conjunction with a parabolic reflector to produce a very tight spot. Although they are being rapidly superseded by halogen projectors, crown-silvered lamps are still a good cheap alternative. The fact that they will only throw light backwards (or downwards) is often neglected; when fitted to a conventional table lamp, for example, they a produce a good, but highly localized, light that is excellent to read by but will not interfere with any other lighting effects in the room.

GLOBES

These are now available as tungsten-filament, halogen and fluorescent lamps. There are a number of luminaires designed specifically to take globe lamps, and their use is largely restricted to situations that exploit their decorative qualities. A globe lamp is also ideal as a replacement for a globe-shape glass shade, especially when it proves difficult to find a suitable substitute for an old one that is broken. Despite appearances, globes do not produce more light than a conventional lamp of the same wattage.

SMALL GLOBES

Small globe lamps are available in all cap sizes, and are very useful for fitting to a luminaire that has a small or very shallow shade, where side glare may be a problem. These lamps are only generally available as clear or pearl, and if a small soft-tone lamp is required, you may have to use a candle lamp.

SOFT-TONE

GLOBES

CANDLE LAMPS IN THEIR PROPER PLACE

FLICKER LAMPS

CANDLE LAMPS

Just like globe lamps, candle lamps are really only decorative, and their use is largely limited to luminaires designed specifically for them. However, they are available in a wider range of colours than small globes, and you can usually substitute one for the other without difficulty.

FLICKER LAMPS

A relatively recent development of the candle lamp, flicker lamps are of no use except for their decorative quality, since they give out no useful light whatsoever. Their intrinsic quality of animation can be put to good use to produce theatrical effects, but do not use them in enclosed reproduction lanterns – the intention of enclosed lanterns was to eliminate flicker and allow the candle to burn steadily, and nothing looks more absurd than this obvious contradiction.

COLOURED LAMPS

Except for the soft-tone lamps, coloured lamps should be reserved for party lighting. The range of colours is limited to a few primary colours, and if you wish to introduce colour into your lighting, filters such as theatre gels are a much better option. Unlike lamps, gel is available in a wide range of colours and will permit much more subtle effects. However, make sure you use specially designed materials which are heatproof.

DAYLIGHT-SIMULATION LAMPS

Despite having bulbs of blue glass, the light from these lamps is very close to real daylight; they were intended for people whose work demands that they can see colours clearly. Daylight-simulation lamps cost a little more than conventional ones, but they are ideal for desks and similar task lighting, or where the simulation of daylight might be useful, as in a conservatory.

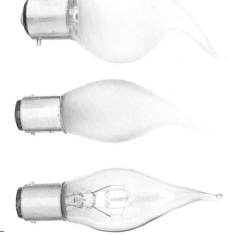

CANDLES & FLAMES

COLOURED GLASS

FLUORESCENTS

THE FLUORESCENT IS THE ONE FORM OF LAMP WHICH IS DESIGNED SPECIFICALLY TO PRODUCE AN ALL-ROUND GLOW. CHEAP TO RUN AND CAPABLE OF PROVIDING A BRIGHT, DIFFUSE LIGHT, THE FLUORESCENT TUBE IS THE MOST COMMON FORM OF LIGHTING IN OUR KITCHENS AND OTHER UTILITY SPACES.

ECONOMY & EFFICIENCY

For economy, the fluorescent cannot be bettered by any other type of lamp, and many of the modern compact fluorescent lamps now available are intended to replace incandescent lamps. They do this very well, having a rated average life (RAL) of 10,000 hours, but they still produce the quality of light distinctive of fluorescent tubes, and many are too big to sit comfortably within a light shade designed for a conventional incandescent lamp. One significant advantage is that they give off very little heat and can, therefore, be used in confined spaces.

THE TUBE

The colour temperature has always been a significant feature of fluorescent tubes. They are standardized now into four types, each intended for use in quite specific circumstances: extra-warm white, warm white, white and cool white. In the USA, all except the warm and cool white have been phased out and eventually only cool white will be available.

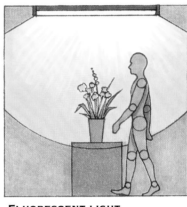

FLUORESCENT LIGHT
This form of lamp provides an economic all-round glow.

COMPACT FLUORESCENTS
These lamps have a rated average life of 10,000 hours.

FLUORESCENT TUBES
The manufacturers of tubes have tended to cater for industrial and commercial needs, and a wide range is available to cover most working environments and conditions.

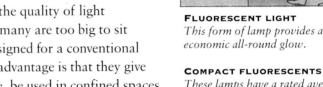

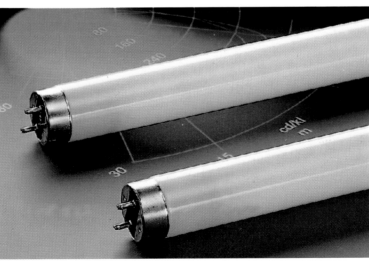

FLUORESCENT TYPES

2D LAMP

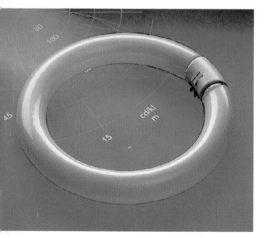

CIRCULAR LAMP

DAYLIGHT-SIMULATION TUBES

Intended mostly for workshops and studios, these serve the same purpose as the incandescent daylight-simulation lamps mentioned previously.

GROWTH-ENHANCING TUBES

This is a highly specialized form of fluorescent lamp, designed specifically to encourage the growth of plants in artificial environments. They are ideal if you use your conservatory for its traditional purpose, but they do not give a very pleasant light to live with.

BLACKLIGHTERS

These are the ultraviolet lamps that make your white shirt glow blue. They are commonly used in nightclubs and similar venues, and can be an amusing feature for a private party, but they should be used sparingly, as prolonged exposure to ultraviolet light can be harmful.

THE 2D LAMP

Designed for use in special luminaires, they have a unique type of cap and you will not fit a conventional luminaire unless you use an adapter. The 2D lamp is ideal for achieving a good broad spread of light.

CIRCULAR FLUORESCENTS

Similar to 2D lamps, circular fluorescents are essentially decorative. They are designed to be used in shallow, round or square luminaires, and are excellent for back-lighting, commonly being used in illuminated signs. Circular fluorescents can be used successfully without any enclosing shade; again, they have their own special type of cap, and can only be used in specific fittings or with an adapter.

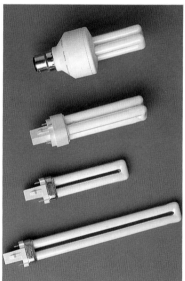

COMPACT BIAXIAL
These lamps are designed to replace incandescents. They are compact fluorescents, available in an increasing variety of shapes and sizes and with various cap types.

PROJECTORS

THESE ARE OFTEN KNOWN AS 'SPOTS', BUT THE TRADE REFERS TO THEM AS PROJECTORS, RESERVING THE WORD 'SPOT' TO DEFINE THE WIDTH OF THE BEAM. IN RECENT YEARS, THE RETAIL BUSINESS HAS TAUGHT US A LOT ABOUT THE VALUE OF DISPLAY LIGHTING, AND MANY DOMESTIC LUMINAIRES NOW AVAILABLE ARE BASED ON THE DESIGN OF COMMERCIAL-DISPLAY LUMINAIRES.

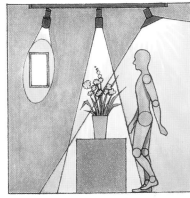

PROJECTION
Originally developed for the theatre.

DOMESTIC 'SPOT' LIGHTING

Projected, or spot, lighting for display purposes was originally developed from theatrical lighting. Put simply, display lighting means using the sort of lamp or lamp/luminaire combination that projects a beam rather than giving an all-round glow. The miniature decorative spot, often available as a unit comprising two or three luminaires, is now in common use and often used to replace an old central pendant.

INTERNAL REFLECTORS

Most projectors for the home have internal reflectors – that is, the inside of the bulb is silvered to concentrate the light and throw it forwards. The width of the beam, from a very narrow spot to a very wide flood, is determined by the shape of the reflector, a wide variety of which is available. The lamps may be described on the package by initials, the most common being:

INTERNAL REFLECTION

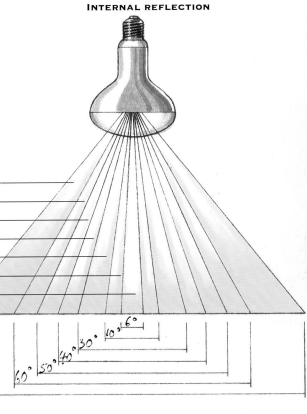

Very wide flood:	VWF	up to 80°
Wide flood:	WF	60 – 70°
Medium flood:	MF	50°
Flood:	F	40°
Spot:	S	30°
Narrow spot:	NSP	10 – 20°
Very narrow spot:	VNSP	down to 6°

Beam
widths 2 →

TYPES OF INTERNAL REFLECTOR

GLS REFLECTOR LAMPS

This is the most common form of projector, available in a wide range of sizes and beam widths, from spot to flood.

SMALL DECORATIVE SPOTS

Increasingly used instead of standard GLS projectors, small decorative spots are common in the home, and there are many luminaires that will accept these lamps. Unfortunately, although the better quality ones are given an RAL of 1000 hours, these small lamps tend to have a very short life span.

DECORATIVE SPOTS

PAR LAMPS

Available as both tungsten-filament and halogen, Parabolic Aluminised Reflector (PAR) lamps are robust internal-reflector lamps with moulded lenses that focus the light into a specific beam. Although common in the USA, in the UK domestic market, PAR lamps tend to be reserved for outdoors, particularly for security luminaires, and there are very few domestic luminaires available for them. Where they are used, they are likely to be in a luminaire intended originally for display and retail lighting, where they are now being superseded by compact halogen systems.

WIDE-ANGLE LAMPS

One recent development is a fluorescent lamp masquerading as a wide-angle projector – they are expensive to install but very cheap to run, and have up to ten times the RAL of a conventional GLS lamp. When I say masquerading, I mean that this is in fact an all-round-glow lamp, but it has a built-in cowl which restricts its beam to 120°.

PAR LAMP

EXTERNAL REFLECTORS

External reflectors have been mostly the preserve of the theatre, cinema and other specialist users; the only place you were likely to find one was in older models of slide projector. The one common exception to this is the external parabolic reflector as part of a specific luminaire.

20 WATT LAMP WITH 13° BEAM ANGLE

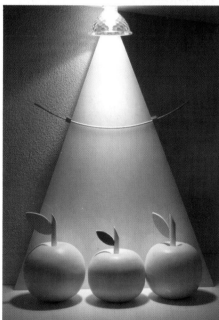

50 WATT LAMP WITH 60° BEAM ANGLE

POWER & BEAM
Projector lamps have always been made with a choice of beam width, shape and power; the final selection depends on what you intend to illuminate. Most lamp manufacturers include this sort of information in their catalogues.

EXTERNAL REFLECTORS

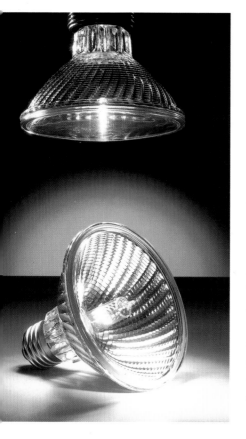

PARABOLIC REFLECTORS

The parabolic reflector is shaped to concentrate light and project it in a very tight beam. It was designed to be used with a crown-silvered lamp which, together, make for a strong spotlight without excessive outlay.

DICHROIC REFLECTORS

Dichroic spot- and floodlamps are fairly recent arrivals from the retail world; you can find any number of shops lit by these discreet but highly efficient lamps. One important distinction between these lamps and conventional ones is that they are powered by a different voltage, usually 12V. The dichroic reflector is a multi-faceted glass bowl, coated in such a way that it projects light forwards but conducts heat backwards. This reflector can either stand alone and be fitted with a separate halogen capsule, or comes with a built-in capsule, sometimes with a glass cover. Although known generically as halogen lamps, the capsule can be filled with other gases, such as xenon.

Halogen-dichroic lamps are ideal for providing a great deal of light exactly where it is wanted, and they, like the GLS lamps, come in a variety of beam widths. They have a long RAL, of up to 3500 hours, and use comparatively little power. However, they may not be cheap to install, and since most of them run on 12V power they require a transformer.

TRANSFORMERS

Transformers for low-voltage luminaires can be either integral or remote. An integral transformer, usually toroidal, is built into the base of the luminaire and, being heavy, has the advantage of making it very stable. Remote transformers are usually much more bulky, and are not intended to be seen. Whether integral or remote, the cost of a transformer makes low-voltage luminaires relatively expensive.

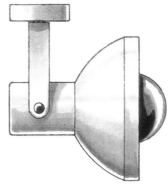

PARABOLIC REFLECTOR

DICHROIC REFLECTOR

HALOGEN CAPSULE

LIGHTING TRACK

LIGHTING TRACK, WHICH IS AVAILABLE IN FREE OR FIXED FORMS, HAS COME DIRECTLY FROM THE DISPLAY AND RETAIL TRADES. THERE IS LOW-VOLTAGE AND MAINS-POWERED LIGHTING TRACK.

FREE TRACK

Track is most useful in its free form – that is as a bus bar into which a luminaire can be fitted at any point. This makes it possible to place a luminaire exactly where it is needed, and allows for a combination of practical and accent lighting, powered and controlled from a single point.

MAINS-VOLTAGE TRACK

This is the traditional track system which has been in use commercially for thirty years or more. In the USA track lighting is often used in the home, but elsewhere it is still relatively uncommon, and mains-voltage track is particularly rare, but it is nonetheless one of the most versatile forms of lighting. Track can be fixed horizontally or vertically, and there is in theory no limit to its length. All systems have corner connectors, some flexible others with fixed angles of 30° or 45°, so it is possible to make up runs that follow a particular line, perhaps around a large room or along a corridor.

LOW-VOLTAGE TRACK

Low-voltage, commonly 12V, free track usually has a remote transformer, perhaps designed to be concealed in the ceiling cavity. The number of luminaires that can be attached to a given length of track depends on the rating of the transformer. For example, one 100VA transformer will run four 20W lamps or two 50W. If you require a long run or more luminaires, you will need additional transformers or you will have to reduce the rating of the lamps. The advantages of low-voltage track are its low running cost and its very compact size. Miniature low-voltage track has been developed for some speciality needs, such as shop-counter display, and this is even more attractive in terms of its weight and scale.

Complex systems of either mains or low-voltage free track will be comparatively complicated to install, and it is best to obtain advice from a specialist, particularly for the fitting.

MAINS-VOLTAGE TRACK
Track installed at picture-rail height illuminates paintings. These luminaires carry internal-reflector GL projectors, but if they are used in this way, they must be of a low wattage to conserve the pictures.

VERSATILITY OF TRACK
A length of track which demonstrates its versatility. While pictures and other art objects around the room are picked out with projector luminaires, the dining table is lit by a pendant suspended from a track adapter.

FIXED TRACK

FIXED SOLUTIONS
Fixed track luminaires and spot clusters, though limited in mobility, can still be adjusted in any direction. Either are good solutions for low budgets, but mains-voltage varieties cannot, as a rule, carry high wattage lamps so you may not be able to illuminate anything at a distance.

FIXED TRACK Many stores now stock a small range of fixed tracks, either 12V or mains-voltage. The low-voltage variety will come with an integral transformer built into the fixing point. Most fixed-track fixtures have three or four luminaires intended to be used with projector lamps, and they will have cowls or external reflectors ready-fitted.

VARIATIONS Nowadays, thanks to the flexibility inherent in fittings, some interesting variations on the lighting track are becoming available, such as slimline track, curved track and even bare-wire systems, but since they are predominantly aimed at the commercial market, they are relatively expensive.

SPOT CLUSTERS Similar to the fixed tracks are the spot clusters. These are a development entirely for the domestic market, and are designed specifically to replace the central ceiling pendant. They are usually mains-voltage and designed to take the miniature decorative spots. These lamps, as we have seen, do tend to suffer from short life span, and this should be borne in mind when fitting luminaires of this sort.

FIXED SPOT CLUSTER

THE POWER OF LIGHT

MODERN DOMESTIC LIGHTING IS 'DRIVEN' BY ELECTRICITY. ELECTRICITY IS A POWERFUL FORCE WHICH SHOULD NOT BE UNDERESTIMATED. INDEED THE TERM 'LA FORCE' IS USED IN THE FRENCH LANGUAGE TO DESCRIBE ELECTRICAL POWER. WHILST A FAITHFUL SERVANT TO MANKIND, ELECTRICITY SHOULD BE TREATED WITH RESPECT. IT PAYS TO SEEK EXPERT ADVICE WHEN INSTALLING OR UPGRADING WIRING, AND TO EXERCISE SIMPLE PRECAUTIONS, EVEN WHEN CHANGING A LIGHT BULB.

ELECTRICAL SAFETY

To the untrained, electricity is dangerous and potentially lethal. No electrical installation, other than the fitting of a plug or a lamp, should be undertaken by an amateur. You should always consult a professional, particularly if your plans are likely to include any rewiring, and remember that it is all too easy to start a fire by incorrect wiring or by overloading a socket.

LIGHT DAMAGE

Watercolours, fabrics and other natural fibres can be destroyed by light. Many people will have experienced their curtains fading and even falling into rags after prolonged exposure to strong sunlight. However, it is not just the sun that will do this; any strong light can damage sensitive materials, and pictures, wallpapers, rugs and so on can fade just like curtains.

This is not a serious problem for most of us, but those people who collect paintings or antique fabrics, for example, should take steps to protect their investments from light damage. The potential for damage can be determined by measuring the lux levels in proximity to them; a safe figure would be well below 50.

One simple expedient would be to ensure they are not placed in direct sunlight, and that they are illuminated indirectly. However, it is the ultraviolet end of the spectrum that is the most damaging for these objects, and anti-UV filters are a must if you intend to light valuable paintings or fabrics for prolonged periods. If you are in any doubt, it would be wise to consult one of the many specialists in the field before exposing valuable items to prolonged harmful light.

LIGHT & CONSERVATION
In this historic house, much care has been taken to reduce the potential damage from light falling on the objects on display. The only items that are lit directly are the pictures, which, being oil paintings, will not be affected by the light. To protect its fabrics and cushions, the sofa is turned with its back to the windows and the picture lights. Modern fabrics are just as susceptible to damage from strong light.

WATTS & VOLTS
To the non-scientist, electricity can be a very difficult concept to grasp, and it is beyond the scope of this book. However, it will be useful to define the common terms in as simple a way as possible, in an effort to avoid confusion. A scientist may not be entirely happy with these definitions, but so be it.

A VOLT: the unit of electromotive force by which your domestic current is measured.

A WATT: the unit of power by which the output of a lamp is determined.

A LUMEN: the unit of light by which the output of a lamp is measured.

LUX: the number of lumens per square metre.

3 CONTROLLING LIGHT

Switching a light on or off is a matter of interrupting the flow of current to the lamp. Wired-in lighting will have a switch on the wall, usually by the door. Self-contained luminaires, such as table lamps, will have a built-in switch, either on the lamp holder itself or fitted to the cable as a torpedo switch. In some circumstances it is possible to have a secondary circuit of sockets, into which you can plug self-contained luminaires, enabling you to control them all from one point; this is common in the USA, but rare in the United Kingdom.

SWITCHING
The level of sophistication applied to light switching depends on budget. Some ideas are easy to accomplish and cost very little.

EASY SWITCHES
Most standard light switches are a small rocker set into a larger faceplate, but some people find these fiddly and awkward to use, and there are places where they are not ideal. Replacing small rocker switches with whole-face rocker switches makes operating them very much easier – it can even be done with an elbow – and it is a good idea in kitchens and workshops where there is water. Do not use them in the bathroom, however; string-pull switches or ground-fault switches are very much safer, and may be a legal or insurance requirement.

Easy switches are also available in two- and three-gang types, so it is quite possible to install them in almost any situation.

AUTOMATIC SWITCHING
Automatic switching is something we could all benefit from, probably more often than we think, and it need not be as complicated and expensive as it sounds.

AUTOMATIC FRIDGE-TYPE SWITCHES
Whenever a house has illuminated storage such as a walk-in pantry or storeroom, it is all too easy to leave the light switched on, an annoyance most people will have experienced. Conversely, it may be that the visit to these spaces is just too brief to bother with switching on a light, even though it would be convenient. In these circumstances an automatic light switch would be ideal, and the cheapest and easiest one to provide is a fridge-type switch. These switches turn on the light when a door is opened and turn it off when the door is closed again. They are simple to install, and can save a disproportionate amount of frustration and electricity.

AUTOMATIC TIME DELAY
There are places where it would be useful to have a light that turns itself off but where a fridge switch would not work. These include places that you may enter through one door and exit through another – halls, corridors and stairways, for example. Wherever a constant light is neither necessary nor desirable, a time-delay switch is ideal. These are often fitted in multi-occupation buildings, but there is no reason why many more people cannot benefit from them.

AUTOMATIC TRIP SWITCHES
Trip switches will do the same job, but without the need for any physical contact at all. These might be triggered by an infrared beam detecting motion or heat, or by breaking a beam of light by walking through it, as with some burglar alarms. There are not many homes which need such a sophisticated system, but very large buildings can benefit greatly from an installation of this sort, particularly with regard to economy.

DIRECT SWITCHING
Many conventional luminaires are fitted with their own switches. These may be an integral part of the lamp holder, or they may be remote 'torpedo' switches fitted to the cable. One major advantage of this sort of switching is its inherent flexibility. You may have as many or as few luminaires on as circumstances demand. In the USA, many integral switches have three positions – on, off and dim, thereby increasing flexibility still further. However, you would be wise to retain at least one light controlled from a switch by the door, to avoid having to fumble about in the dark.

CIRCUITS

One of the main themes of this book is the creation of mood and atmosphere, and once the lighting is on, a different sort of control may be useful. Some rooms might benefit from different atmospheres at different times; breakfast and dinner would make quite different demands on the lighting in a dining room, for example.

MULTI-CIRCUITS

One simple way to achieve different lighting arrangements would be to have two or more circuits switched independently, to provide a variety of light levels and moods. An example might be circuit 1 for the accent light, circuits 1 and 2 for general, ambient light, and circuit 2 alone for practical light. Used in conjunction with a dimmer switch, even more control is possible.

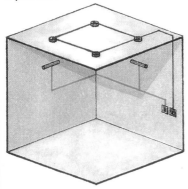

EXAMPLE OF A MULTI-CIRCUIT
Circuit 1 serves the wall-mounted picture lights and circuit 2 serves the recessed ceiling down-lighters.

DIMMED LIGHTING

Not all forms of lighting can be dimmed. Some low-voltage and some fluorescent lamps are not suitable, although any conventional domestic filament lamp can be dimmed. A good lamp stockist will be able to advise you on this.

DIMMER SWITCHES
The dimmer switches sold in electrical and hardware stores as simple replacements for conventional switches usually have a low power rating. Consequently, it is not possible to control more than one or two luminaires at time – usually a central pendant and perhaps a pair of wall lights. Also, low-priced dimmer fittings tend to be quite noisy, giving off an annoying buzz that gets louder the lower you turn down the light.

If your budget will stretch to it, there are commercial control systems of varying complexity available, any of which will overcome these problems, but they will certainly require professional installation.

SECURITY LIGHTING

There are not many people who will want to fit fully automatic switches simply for lighting, but they do have significant advantages for security. (See also page 145.)

(See also page 145.)

HEAT OR MOTION TRIGGERS
We are all familiar with exterior systems where heat or motion will trigger a light, and they are becoming a standard feature of basic domestic security. However, on the principle that to deter an intruder from entering is better than trying to lock him out, the appearance of occupation is one very effective trick. Neither of the ideas below need be expensive, and yet the combination might go a long way to prevent a break-in.

TRIP SWITCHES
Installing a trip switch outside the house to control a light or a group of lights on the inside is not a familiar idea, but would be most effective in raising doubt in the mind of a potential intruder.

TIMERS
Similarly, timed lighting can give the appearance of occupation, even over a prolonged period. Installing a timer that can be programmed in a way similar to a central-heating system, can provide the necessary variation to any automatic lighting to fool at least casual inspection.

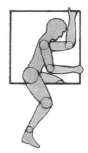

BUILT-IN SECURITY SENSORS
In this porch, black-aluminium and glass lanterns, fitted with auto-sensors, complement the traditional and 'homely' feel of the house and provide security at the same time.

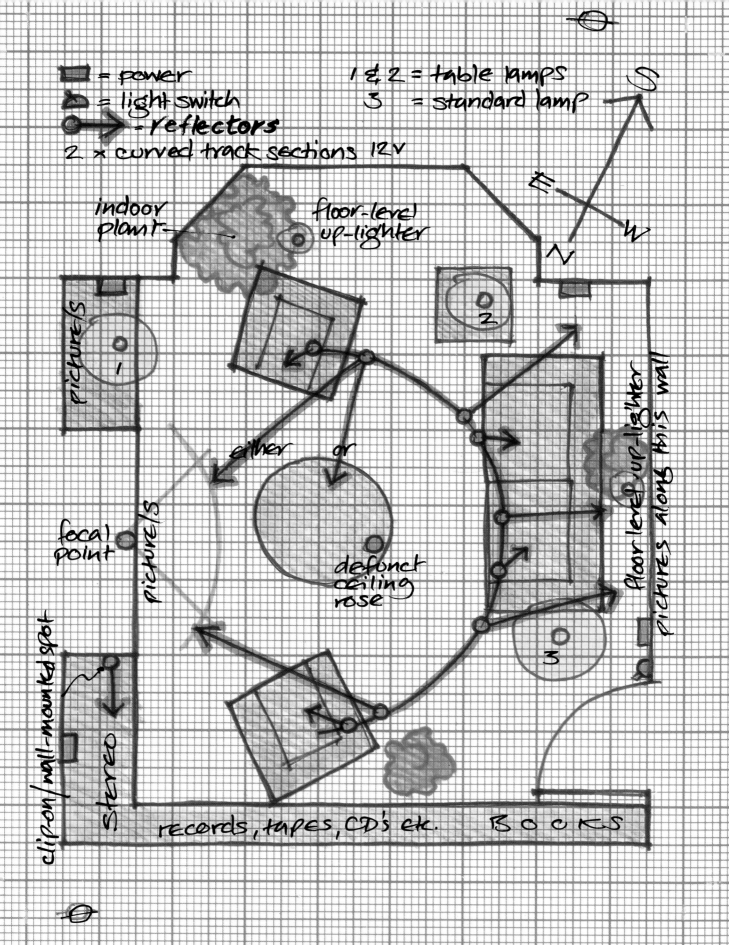

= power   1 & 2 = table lamps

= light switch   3 = standard lamp

= reflectors

2 × curved track sections 12v

indoor plant

floor-level up-lighter

pictures/s

1

either

or

focal point

pictures/s

defunct ceiling rose

2

floor level up-lighter

pictures along this wall

3

clip-on/wall-mounted spot

stereo

records, tapes, CD's etc.   B O O K S

PLANNING YOUR LIGHTING

NOW THAT WE HAVE COVERED THE PRINCIPLES OF LIGHT AND HOW IT IS PRODUCED, IT IS TIME TO MOVE ON TO HOW WE MIGHT USE IT, AND HOW WE GO ABOUT CREATING MOODS AND ATMOSPHERES TO SUIT EACH OF US IN OUR OWN HOMES, YET IN A WAY THAT CONTINUES TO CATER FOR OUR PRACTICAL NEEDS.

In order to plan your lighting, irrespective of which room you are intending to light, you need to understand exactly how you intend to use that space. The first step, therefore, is to take a space and analyze its shape, size and uses. To help with this process, illustrated on the left is a hypothetical room – in this case a sitting room. The dimensions and essential features such as doors and windows have been noted and the uses have been listed in order of priority.

Remember, this example is a theoretical analysis and any or all of the uses listed may be quite different from your own needs and circumstances. So make your own list – you will be surprised how useful it will be – and draw your plan as accurately to scale as possible. Making your sketch on squared paper will be enormously helpful.

PLANNING CHECKLIST

DIMENSIONS OF ROOM & ESSENTIAL FEATURES

Shape: roughly square

Size: 4m (13ft) x 4.5m (15ft)

Ceiling height: 3.05m (10ft)

No. of windows: one, large bay

Aspect: south, south-east

Fireplace: yes

CONTENTS OF ROOM

Stereo

Books

Paintings

Some sculpture

Three decorative lamps

MAIN USES OF THE ROOM

Reading

Listening to music

Conversation

Entertaining small numbers

Occasional card or other table-top games

Occasional party

LIKELY NUMBER OF PERSONS

Four, expanding to six from time to time

By making such a list, it is possible to identify a number of important factors that will affect the way a room might be arranged and lit.

DRAWING A ROOM PLAN
Take the dimensions of the room, including the ceiling height. Note all the existing features and light sources. Transferring your dimensions to squared paper will give you a fairly accurate scale plan.

THE CHOICE IS YOURS
No lighting retailer, even one that stocks an extensive range, will be able to choose your lighting for you. You can certainly seek advice on wattage, voltage and so on, but make your plans in advance and only then go shopping to find luminaires that will fulfil your specific needs.

VERSATILE LIGHTING
A low-voltage track system enables you to put light where you need it without overpowering the room.

LIGHTING TO READ BY
This length of curved track is ideal for light to read by. Each of the small, unobtrusive luminaires throws a tightly focused beam onto each chair. Further accent lighting is provided by the scattering of table lamps, which also serve to soften any hardness in the spot light.

SPECIFIC POINTS

We know that the fireplace is likely to form the focal point of the room, since it will have no competition from a television set. This particular room may be very sunny during the morning and at midday, but will receive little or no afternoon sunlight.

We also know that a good deal of shelving will be required for books, records, tapes and CDs, and that some wall space will have to be reserved for pictures. As a consequence, little actual wall area is likely to be exposed, and what there is would best be painted or covered in a pale colour to prevent the room from becoming too dark.

In addition, good reading light will be required for four people; however, we don't want to use too many free-standing luminaires because the space will be needed for seating guests and for occasional parties.

SUGGESTIONS & SOLUTIONS

One possible solution can be found in the photograph (above right). Two sections of curved track will provide the opportunity to direct good reading light to each of the seats, without the need for extra table or standing lamps; the track could be powered from the ceiling rose, and could thus be controlled from the door. It also allows lighting to be projected onto pictures. Using track provides flexibility, so that lighting can be added or moved when you rearrange furniture and pictures.

A clip-on spot could supply light for the stereo equipment and, for atmosphere, you could include free-standing floor-level up-lighters, one perhaps shining up through an indoor plant.

Drawing up a list that helps you understand how a room will be used, when it will be used, and by how many people, makes it easier to plan the lighting. Other factors, such as the need for extra power points, may also be identified at this stage.

Don't reserve this exercise just for the sitting room – any room in the house, even the garden, can and should be planned in this way. Until you know how a space will be used, you cannot plan a sensible and effective lighting scheme.

USING TABLE LAMPS
The conventional solution would be to use the table lamps themselves, although they may not be convenient for all.

WHEN LIGHTING YOUR HOME, YOU WILL BE FACED WITH MANY MORE CHOICES THAN YOU MIGHT ANTICIPATE, AND THERE ARE SOME FUNDAMENTAL QUESTIONS YOU SHOULD ASK YOURSELF BEFORE STARTING. IS THE PERIOD OF THE HOUSE IMPORTANT? WHAT IS THE QUALITY OF THE AVAILABLE NATURAL LIGHT, AND HOW CAN IT BEST BE EXPLOITED? IS THE INTENTION TO TACKLE ONE ROOM OR THE WHOLE HOUSE? A LOT DEPENDS ON HOW FAR YOU WANT TO GO AND HOW MUCH YOU ARE PREPARED TO SPEND; WHATEVER THE SCALE, IT IS BEST NOT TO START UNTIL YOU HAVE THE ANSWERS.

CHAPTER FOUR
LIGHTING ROOM BY ROOM

65

WHAT DO I WANT?

ONE OF THE MOST BASIC QUESTIONS IS 'WHAT DO I WANT TO DO IN THIS ROOM?'. UNTIL YOU KNOW YOU REALLY CANNOT PROCEED, SO START BY LISTING THE SPECIFIC ACTIVITIES ROOM BY ROOM. THE ANSWERS ARE NOT ALWAYS OBVIOUS, AND SOME MAY BE SURPRISING. LIGHT FALLS INTO TWO BASIC CATEGORIES, PRACTICAL AND ACCENT, EITHER OF WHICH CAN BE DIRECT OR INDIRECT, AND EACH AREA OF THE HOUSE WILL REQUIRE A DIFFERENT BALANCE.

PRACTICAL LIGHT

Practical light is that which enables you to do things, and there are right and wrong ways of providing it. This is task-and-activity lighting, and if a light is badly placed or of the wrong type for its intended job, it is not practical. Function is what defines practical light, and its success or failure is easy to evaluate by simply asking the question, does it help you to do the task or activity for which it was intended?

ACCENT LIGHT

Accent light, while it may contribute some practical light, is more to do with creativity and imagination. It is the accent light that does most to create an atmosphere. The two are not, of course, mutually exclusive, but it makes planning considerably easier to consider them separately.

AMBIENT LIGHT

The amount of ambient light provided by the combination of practical and accent lighting is what defines a space as being dim or bright. Ambient light is the overall quantity and quality of the light in a room. Depending on the function of the space being lit, more or less ambient light will be required; the level and quality of the ambient light define the atmosphere.

IDENTIFYING LIGHT
Left: Practical light illuminates the desk top, while accent light accentuates the wall display. These specific sources of illumination, together with light from other sources such as a central down-lighter, combine to make the ambient light in the room.

LIGHTING TYPES IN USE

Top left: A good example of accent lighting – the strong bookshelf lighting provides adequate ambient light.
Bottom left: The task lighting installed beneath the wall units in this kitchen fulfils a similar function.
Below: In most cases, however, a single source is insufficient, and supplementary lighting is required. This breakfast table has good task light from the pendant, combined with natural light from the window.

67

4 ACHIEVING ATMOSPHERE

A RELAXING ATMOSPHERE, FOR MOST OF US, IS LIKELY TO BE
CREATED BY SEVERAL DIM LIGHTS RATHER THAN A FEW BRIGHT
ONES. REMEMBER, ALTHOUGH A SINGLE 100W CENTRAL PENDANT
LAMP WILL ILLUMINATE THE ROOM; SIX SCATTERED 40W LAMPS
WILL GIVE YOU NEARLY TWICE AS MUCH LIGHT, BUT OF A QUITE
DIFFERENT AND MORE COMFORTABLE KIND.

DEFINING ATMOSPHERE

It is predominantly accent light which defines atmosphere, but
the quality of atmosphere depends on personal taste, and here
there are no solutions, only suggestions. Try to stop thinking
about lights as things bought from a store and start thinking
about light as something to be played with. This is light for its
own sake; it can be direct or indirect, plain, coloured, static or
in motion. It can flood a surface or pick out details; it can bring
out, or even create, form. It should be thought of as almost
sculptural and used with as much imagination as possible.

COMMON TECHNIQUES

The most common form of general lighting is the central
pendant, a light that is switched on and off from the door.
Despite its ubiquity and obvious convenience, it is not always
the best solution. If it is bright enough to provide useful light,
then it is usually too bright to allow any subtlety of
atmosphere. Rooms lit this way tend to take on the feel of a
waiting room, no matter what other forms of lighting are
provided. In truth, the central pendant is a survivor from the
earliest days of electric lighting.

When electricity was replacing gas and oil as a clean and
controllable means to extend the hours of daylight, the choices
available were limited in the extreme. In those days, it was
generally a pendant luminaire or nothing, and this idea has
never entirely disappeared.

Of course, there are circumstances where the pendant, in one
form or another, is exactly what is needed. If the house has a
strong period feel, and you want to preserve or re-create an
authentic atmosphere, there is a wide choice of suitable pendant
luminaires available.

CENTRAL PENDANTS
*Central pendants, which provide the
main illumination for this dining
room, are supported by accent
lighting from the floor-level up-
lighters and candles on the table. This
combination provides a good level of
ambient light and enhances the
elegant decorative style of the room.*

A SIMPLE SOLUTION
Top: The table light is probably the most familiar form of lighting after the central pendant. A number of well-chosen table and standard lights will often provide all the illumination you need, and there are styles to suit any interior scheme.
Below: Lighting track is, perhaps, the most flexible form of lighting. It gives you the opportunity to put light exactly where you need it. In this case, light is projected onto both walls and the table top, but the luminaires can always be moved if necessary, and they can all be turned on or off together.

SOME BASIC SOLUTIONS

The simple solution would be table lights or standard lights. Their shades add their own colour and atmosphere to the room, and should be considered as part of the overall decorative scheme. Miniature spotlights, clamped to convenient places, can direct light into awkward corners and are very effective for providing both practical and accent light.

Multiple-source lighting in this form is the usual answer, reached by most people without a great deal of thought. But this approach does incur problems. Many of the luminaires and shades available are far from practical and are only intended for accent lighting. There are some places where it will be impossible to provide a light without wires trailing about the floor or by over-using a wall socket. Both practices are highly dangerous, and it may not be possible to turn any of the lights on or off from the door without at least some rewiring.

LIGHTING TRACK

This enables you to place a luminaire and direct a controlled beam wherever it is needed. There are plenty of modern track systems which are neither difficult nor expensive to install, and they can often be powered from an existing central pendant fixture controlled from the doorway, thus avoiding rewiring. Many stores stock a small range of useful 'fixed' tracks and spot clusters, all of which have their uses, but lighting track is really useful when it is in its 'free' form, enabling one to place a luminaire exactly where it is needed.

With the constant development of low-voltage luminaires, some interesting variations on the lighting track are becoming available such as curved slim-line track, parallel bare-wire systems, and complex plug-in systems. However, since most of these are aimed predominantly at the commercial market, they are relatively expensive. Track lighting is not a solution on its own. It is essentially only down-light, and is best used with other 'effect' lighting. Don't feel constrained by the 'squareness' of the room; track placed on the diagonal will often be more effective than if it runs parallel with the walls.

STRIP LIGHTING

This comparatively small room has been made to feel much larger by covering one wall entirely with mirror glass and by installing a continuous run of fluorescent tube around the skylight. The latter provides a wash of diffuse light while the inherent harshness is softened by concealing it in a recess.

STRIP LIGHTING

Valued mostly for its prodigious output, the inherent power-economy of fluorescent light is becoming increasingly important. However, because of its colour and diffuse nature, the light is very harsh and tends to eliminate nearly all shadow. As a result, the ambient light is very bland, the opposite of what we are seeking to achieve. The fluorescent tube is best reserved for situations where quantity of light is the main objective, such as in workshops and storerooms.

Other forms of fluorescent lamp can provide economy and atmosphere, though they must be used with care. Many shades designed for filament lamps will not fit even a compact fluorescent lamp, so your choice may be limited. A fluorescent gives a much whiter and more intense light than a filament lamp and, to avoid it dominating the room, it should be given a shade of an appropriate colour, translucency and shape.

FIXED DOWN-LIGHTERS

In a period house, the inevitable modernity of track lighting may be obtrusive and spoil the feeling of a room. Free-standing table or standard lamps may not provide all the light that is needed, and a good solution might be down-lighters. Installed onto or recessed into the ceiling, they are discreet and usually can be switched on and off from a single point by the door. The main disadvantage with down-lighters is that, once installed, they can't be moved easily, and it is then difficult to change the layout of the room. Installing directional down-lighters, with which the light need not be aimed straight downwards, will provide at least some degree of flexibility.

ACCENT DOWN-LIGHT

Left: The dramatic use of down-light picks out a specific item, creating a focal point while providing a good level of ambient light. The mirror doubles the effect.

DOWN-LIGHTING

Above: Recessed down-lighters are an unobtrusive means of providing illumination for a room whatever period or style predominates. In this case, directional down-lighters offer a more flexible use of illumination to highlight selected objects and spaces.

71

4 CONTROLLING ATMOSPHERE

The ideal system offers control over the sort of lighting and atmosphere needed for any occasion. Flexibility can be achieved by various means other than simply providing each luminaire with a switch. A bank of switches by the door, for example, could be wired to control different combinations of luminaires within the room. One switch could control a central luminaire via a dimmer, another could operate a number of wall lights, and so on.

FLEXIBLE STRATEGIES

The number of groups controlled in this way depends on the complexity of the wiring and the size of the room, but two would be adequate for most rooms. Commercial systems allow for a high degree of control – each switch with its own dimming capability, for example. The more elaborate will provide automatic switching of selected groups of luminaires to a pre-set output level, at the push of a button. However, these systems are expensive to purchase and install.

To do any flexible switching properly, it is necessary to start from scratch and install special wiring. Here the wisest course would be to consult specialists, particularly for the actual installation. No electrical wiring should be carried out by non-professionals; it is dangerous, and illegal in many countries.

DUAL SYSTEMS

In any rewiring scheme, it is worth considering a dual-socket system whereby the wall sockets are doubled, with one that can be switched remotely from the door. This solution will be more or less possible, depending on which mains voltage is standard. North America, for example, operates on a 120V system and dual-sockets are common, whereas the UK operates on 240V and has no tradition of remote-socket switching.

The most important feature of a system of this sort is that the power and light sockets must not be confused with one another. Such an installation in the UK could output the lighting circuit through small round-pin sockets, for example. Wherever you are, you should consult a professional to ascertain local conditions and law. Ignoring local regulations

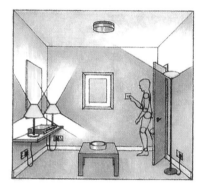

DUAL CIRCUITS
The dual circuit is a method often used in North America where one half of each double socket is linked to a lighting circuit and controlled from a switch by the door. The integral switch of each luminaire still permits individual control when circumstances require it, but generally, one set-up serves for all.

PRESERVING THE ATMOSPHERE

Those seeking to create an ideal set-up will want to preserve the arrangement and switch them all on and off together. This combination of wall-mounted and standard up-lighters creates a pleasant atmosphere, with sufficient ambient light. This arrangement would be an ideal candidate for a dual circuit.

may, at the very least, invalidate building and contents insurance. Both systems present us with the optimum solution, which is a fully controllable lighting scheme. A system such as this allows for much more flexible illumination without us having to fumble in the dark for a table-light switch, with all the attendant hazards.

ACCENT LIGHT

ONCE THE PRACTICAL PROBLEMS HAVE BEEN OVERCOME, IT IS TIME FOR THE SPECIAL EFFECTS. REMEMBER THAT THE PRACTICAL LIGHT MAY NOT PROVIDE THE LIGHT QUALITY THAT YOU SEEK, AND VERY OFTEN IT IS THE ADDITION OF ACCENT LIGHTING WHICH PROVIDES THE ATMOSPHERE. IT IS IMPOSSIBLE TO SEPARATE PRACTICAL LIGHT FROM ACCENT LIGHT, BUT THINKING OF THEM AS SEPARATE IDEAS MAKES THE INITIAL PLANNING STAGES EASIER.

HIGH-LEVEL UP-LIGHT
Up-lighting installed at picture-rail level, or above, will lift the ceiling visually and make a small room appear larger. In this kitchen, the blend of up-light, natural light and recessed task light provides atmosphere in a working environment.

UP-LIGHTERS

Any suitably shaped luminaire with a projector lamp or one that is appropriately shaded can be used as an up-lighter, as can a clip-on spotlight – useful for throwing light upwards into corners. Up-lighters can be placed on the floor or fixed to the wall, and will provide a quite different feel depending on the height at which they are mounted.

More and more, wall-mounted up-lighters are becoming popular; mounted above eye level, they throw a fan of light towards the ceiling and are used increasingly in foyers and atria. There is a good variety of luminaires of this sort specifically aimed at the domestic market, often with shades that can be painted to match or complement a specific décor.

PICTURE-RAIL UP-LIGHTERS

A dramatic effect can be created by installing a continuous, or apparently continuous, strip of light at picture-rail height. Because of the cold nature of fluorescent light, it is possible to fit these strips very close to surfaces and to give them close-fitting shades without damaging the walls or creating a fire risk. This will have the effect of raising the ceiling and making the room appear much higher and airier – it is a technique often used in commercial premises to introduce an air of grandeur.

FLOOR-LEVEL UP-LIGHTERS

Luminaires specifically intended to be used as floor-level up-lighters are rarer, but they are worth seeking out as they can provide some very dramatic effects – for example, a luminaire placed on the floor behind an indoor plant will project the pattern of foliage onto the wall and ceiling. Floor- or low-level up-lighters are particularly good at illuminating dark corners.

LOW-LEVEL UP-LIGHT
This group of objects illustrates the dramatic use of up-light to provide accent. The light from the window throws the sculpture into relief, while the floor-level up-lighter gives the whole group a three-dimensional quality.

**PRACTICAL LIGHTING
USED FOR ACCENT**

*Installing concealed lamps in a
display case, serves two needs. The
objects are well illuminated and the
light created adds to the level of
ambient light in the room. Note in
this picture that, while the collection
of ceramic ware is nicely lit, the
reflections in the glass are
overpowering. Try to achieve an
acceptable balance between the light
inside and outside of a showcase.*

DISPLAY LIGHTING

Most of us associate display lighting more with art galleries or
retail stores than houses, but it can apply equally well at home.
Lighting a picture or a specialist collection is essentially display
lighting, but, though it is not task lighting, it has a practical
application and can be provided by the same means, such as
track-mounted projectors or directional down-lighters.

Dedicated picture lights, which are mounted to the wall
above a picture and provide local focused light, are readily
available. The one possible drawback to using these is that you
have to be sure that you will always want a picture in that space,
since picture lights have to be hard-wired into the wall.

A serious collector may want to buy special display
showcases; many of these will have some form of lighting built
in, which will both light the collection and contribute to the
overall ambient light level within the room.

DRAMATIC LIGHT

THERE ARE MANY IDEAS THAT CAN BE GLEANED FROM COMMERCIAL PREMISES, SHOPS AND RESTAURANTS BEING GOOD EXAMPLES; SOME OF THE MOST SPECTACULAR EFFECTS CAN BE ACHIEVED BY USING TECHNIQUES ADAPTED FROM THE THEATRE.

PROJECTION

The slide projector is usually thought of as something we use to show our holiday slides and then put back in the cupboard until next year, but with suitable space, projecting an image onto an available wall will both add to the ambient light and be spectacular and arresting to look at. This could be a changeable 'window' onto a favourite view, or simply an abstract pattern. It is important not to confuse the two uses of the word projector. For most people a projector is a means to throw a still or moving image onto a screen or wall. However, in the lighting trade, the word projector is used to describe a lamp designed to throw a beam of light in one direction only.

ANIMATION

One common theatrical use of the projected image is the 'gobo'. Mounted over a spot projector, this is usually a disc of fine aluminium with a pattern or design cut out of it to make a silhouette. Gobos are used singly or with a colour filter, or are sometimes animated by having a second, special, gobo mounted to a small motor, causing it to revolve and produce various visual effects like smoke, fire, running water, clouds, and so on.

While there are miniature theatre luminaires available that would be suitable for domestic use, this would be beyond most home-lighting budgets. But animation is a particularly good way to produce interesting and pleasing special effects, and the more standard luminaires are not the only way to achieve it.

ANIMATION
The heat rising from the lamp causes the fan to rotate, thus casting shadows that move in a circular pattern. When this combination of light and shadow is projected through something like a cut-out, a piece of textured glass or a plant, it creates a dramatic display of shadows in motion.

FLAME EFFECTS

Electric fires with a flame effect are in fact using a form of animated gobo, except that in this case, the motion is generated by the heat of the lamp. Experimenting with this idea can produce some good, fun effects, but be certain to use inflammable materials and do not compromise the safety of the luminaire used for the light source.

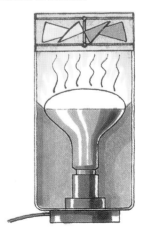

THE DRAMA OF SHADOW

*Projecting light past or through
something can create dramatic
contrasts of light and shade. This
sense of drama can be achieved by
the careful positioning of the light
source, as in the picture to the left,
but you can achieve more elaborate
effects by such means as projecting
the light through coloured filters, as
in the picture below.*

COLOUR & TONE

ONE VERY IMPORTANT THING TO REMEMBER IS THAT THE COLOUR OF THE LIGHT ITSELF HAS A PROFOUND EFFECT ON THE ATMOSPHERE. THIS MAY BE PROVIDED BY A COLOURED OR DECORATED SHADE, BUT IT IS THE LAMP ITSELF WHICH REALLY DECIDES THE COLOUR OF THE LIGHT.

CHOOSING LAMPS   Nowadays the choice is very much wider than the plain or pearl lamps of various wattages that most of us have been used to; there is an increasing range of lamps with muted tones and subtle colours, and the quality of light will be determined as much by these as anything. Simply changing all the 100W lamps in a room to 40W toned lamps will have a dramatic effect on the quality of light and the electricity bill.

THE COLOUR OF LIGHT
The colour of the light, whether it is provided by the lamp glass or by the shade itself, has a profound effect on the atmosphere. In this picture, the room is given a cool and calm atmosphere by the green glass of the light shade.

SETTING THE TONE

The choice of luminaire and lamp are as important as the décor itself in influencing the colour and thus the tone of a room. In the picture left, a warm effect is created by the combination of the paints and fabrics, and the use of soft-tone lamps and warm-yellow shades to the table lights. In the picture below, the opposite effect is achieved by using high-level up-lighters on white-painted walls and the dramatic contrast of the black seat with its white cushion.

79

ALTERNATIVES

THESE DAYS IT IS AXIOMATIC THAT LIGHT EQUALS ELECTRICITY, AND IT MAY BE THOUGHT PERVERSE TO RE-INTRODUCE OLDER FORMS OF LIGHTING INTO A MODERN HOME. IF YOU INTEND TO ACHIEVE A SUBTLE AND WELCOMING ATMOSPHERE, HOWEVER, THE OLDER FORMS OF LIGHT CAN COME IN VERY USEFUL. THE LIGHT GIVEN BY EARLIER FORMS OF LAMP WAS QUITE DIFFERENT IN COLOUR AND TONE TO THOSE POWERED BY ELECTRICITY.

CANDLES & OIL LAMPS

Some of the quietest and most pleasant effect lighting can be provided by oil lamps or candles combined with focused directional light. Nowadays there are many specialist shops selling candles and candle holders of all shapes and sizes – plain, scented, coloured, festive, decorative and plain practical.

Practical oil lamps and the fuel they burn (actually paraffin or kerosene) may be more difficult to find, but suppliers do still exist and it is well worth the effort of seeking one out. There is also a wide choice of shade available for oil lamps, usually made of coloured or plain glass, often etched or cut. Most oil lamps are copies of eighteenth- and nineteenth-century originals, and a polished brass oil lamp with a glowing glass shade would be an attractive addition to any traditionally furnished room.

WINDOW SHADES & BLINDS
The dining table in this room is lit by a pendant luminaire hung from a track, but, during the day, the white venetian blind is ideal for directing the available natural light onto the table top and providing a pleasing, cool atmosphere overall.

NATURAL LIGHT

Don't forget the light outside. Although we tend to think of lighting as something that happens at night, this is far from true. Many rooms are naturally dim – perhaps because they face north, or because the windows are heavily shaded by trees or other buildings. The atmosphere in a room and how much artificial light is needed during the daytime will be greatly affected by how you deal with the light coming in from outside.

WINDOW SHADES

How, or even if, you curtain off the windows will have a profound effect on the feel of a room at all times of the day. The choice of curtains, blinds, nets and so on is beyond the scope of this book, but do consider it and include it when planning a lighting scheme.

NATURAL LIGHT

Left: Again, the use of window shading helps to create the atmosphere. The fine net curtains in this bedroom, in combination with the up-lighting, give an atmosphere redolent of peace and comfort. Small table lights at the bedside cater for the occupant's needs, and the mirror serves to enlarge the space.

CANDLELIGHT

Right: The quiet, intimate atmosphere of this room is achieved with a clever combination of heavy décor and lighting. Practical illumination is provided by the picture light and table light, but the candle holders do much to enhance the impression. The candles are artificial in this instance, but the effect would be the same were they the real thing and they would provide as much light.

ENTRANCES

ALL TOO OFTEN LIT ONLY FOR UTILITY, THE ENTRANCE TO YOUR HOME SAYS A GREAT DEAL ABOUT YOU AND THE WELCOME THAT YOU GIVE. SINCE VERY FEW PEOPLE NEED TO PERFORM TASKS IN THE ENTRANCE, THE ONLY PRACTICAL REQUIREMENT IS ENOUGH LIGHT TO SEE BY. THIS LIGHTING IS ESSENTIALLY FOR ATMOSPHERE, ALLOWING THE ACCENT LIGHTING TO PROVIDE THE NECESSARY AMBIENT LIGHT LEVEL.

THE LIGHT OUTSIDE
Opposite: What more welcome sight than the lights of home at the end of the day. One carefully positioned up-lighter is all this town house needs both to identify itself and to welcome a visitor. Added drama is provided by strong shadows cast by the porch.

OUTSIDE

Outdoor lighting is discussed in Chapter 5, but it is worth noting something here about the light outside the front door. There are two things entrance light should do: one is to identify the house, and the other is to allow easy approach to the door. Provided the distance is not excessive, lighting the porch or the outside of the door may answer both needs. There is a wide choice of exterior luminaires available, ranging from a carriage lamp to a simple bulkhead luminaire, and the choice will depend on the period of the building and personal taste.

INSIDE

Commonly, entrance halls and staircases will have a switch by the main door with perhaps another by the sitting room and another upstairs, all switching the same light or group of lights, usually central pendants. This arrangement is very sensible and should not be disturbed, but the luminaires certainly can be.

THE FOCAL POINT

Halls and stairwells usually lack a focal point, and consequently are not easy to define as spaces. In addition to any display lighting or up-lighting you have planned, a single shaded table light will give a warm focal point and go a long way towards establishing a warm welcoming atmosphere.

A FOCAL POINT
This group of table light and dried flowers creates a focal point to the room and illuminates the entrance. The choice of luminaire and shade expresses something about the mood of the home, while the fabric of the shade brings out the warm tone of the décor.

DISPLAY

An entrance hall is often a prime place for hanging pictures. Replacing one or more of the pendant luminaires with spot clusters or fixed track will enable you to show off your pictures and still provide enough ambient light for practical purposes. Take care when positioning lights in relation to glazed pictures – if they are badly placed, they may produce reflections.

A CONTRAST OF STYLES

Left: A simple group of table, objects and picture are enough to create a focal point and provide interest to what otherwise might be a dull space. This particular table light is ideal for this group since it casts light downwards onto the table, upwards onto the picture and has a shade that throws a pleasant glow into the room.

Right: Different situations demand different solutions. This very narrow space is intelligently lit, using a pendant enhanced by daylight from the fanlight, while the corridor effect is diminished by wall lights in the recess. Just like a mirror, this illumination makes the space feel wider that it really is.

MAKING A GRAND ENTRANCE

Everything in this room helps to strengthen its sense of grandeur. The colours, the materials and the objects all express opulence, as do the tall, elegant table lights. Their thin-fabric shades allow strong accent light and the shadows they cast both up and down provide interest. Additional light is supplied by subtle recessed down-lighters.

THE MIXTURE
It is often a mixture that creates the required effect. In this corner at the foot of the stairs, a heavily shaded table light creates an intimate focal point, the mirror behind both enlarges the space and borrows light by reflecting the up-lighter opposite. A dim overhead light brings out the pictures, and natural light from a window behind the camera throws reflections off the chest of drawers.

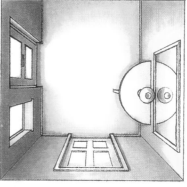

BORROWING LIGHT
Placing a mirror opposite a window will reflect the natural light, thereby doubling its effect and serving to make the space appear wider. At night, a similar effect can be achieved by placing a table light directly in front of the mirror.

UP-LIGHTING

Entrance halls and stairwells can benefit greatly from up-lighting. It is a very common practice in commercial buildings, and gives a light, airy feel to the space. That impression is dependent on the height of the luminaires. Generally, the lower they are mounted the gentler the effect, so experiment with the height before making a final decision. Remember that wall lights will need rewiring, whereas you can power free-standing up-lighters from a socket.

BORROWED LIGHT

Many entrance halls suffer from a lack of natural light, and it pays to make the best of what is available. A large mirror, or a number of small ones carefully placed, can give the illusion of more light, since they make the space feel larger. If it is possible, put a mirror opposite any natural light source so that it can reflect the light directly. A mirror is just as useful at night to reflect a table light, for example, making the entire space much more interesting.

COLOURED GLASS

Many older houses have doors made with coloured-glass panels or a similar fanlight above. Either is a bonus, since it brings a variety of coloured light into a room. Coloured and stained glass appear mostly in houses of the nineteenth and early twentieth centuries, but there is no reason why a suitable picture or abstract design cannot be fitted to a house of any period, and into almost any room. During the day it adds a whole new dimension to the light inside, and it glows beautifully at night.

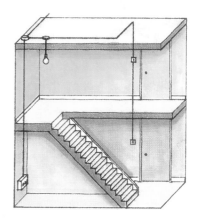

MULTI-SWITCHED CONTROL
A typical arrangement for switching the lights on and off from more than one level. In this case one luminaire can be controlled from two places.

SITTING ROOMS

THE SITTING ROOM IS THE PLACE IN WHICH WE RELAX, YET THE GENERAL TERM COVERS A WIDE RANGE OF ACTIVITIES, INCLUDING ENTERTAINING GUESTS, READING, LISTENING TO MUSIC, PLAYING GAMES, OR WATCHING TELEVISION, EACH OF WHICH HAS PARTICULAR DEMANDS ON THE LIGHTING.

FUNCTION & ATMOSPHERE

The sitting room is thus one of the more challenging spaces to light, since its needs to combine both functional and atmospheric lighting, both of which may be required at the same time. None of the list of possible uses to which we might put our sitting room are mutually exclusive, but many do demand specific lighting conditions to be enjoyable or even possible. Choosing a favourite tape or disc from a rack in the darkest corner of the room can be awkward, and most people have had the experience of having to re-arrange the seating to be able to read a newspaper comfortably. The sitting room is also often the place that reflects most strongly the personality of the house, and is a likely candidate for special-effect lighting.

A PLACE TO RELAX
Opposite: The mixture of light sources combined with natural daylight enhances the sympathetic colours of the décor and fabrics to create a relaxing environment while providing for the practical needs of the occupants.

PERIOD HOMES

If you have an older property and want to preserve or re-create its period atmosphere, it may be possible to find luminaires that reflect that impression. What you use depends on the period of your home, the décor of the room and the effect you want to create, but be aware that in a house dating from before the invention of electric or gas lighting, it will be very difficult not to produce a pastiche, and any installation using 'period' lighting must be done with caution. The spotlight is essentially modern, and lighting to period will always produce better results if it is thought of as decorative rather than practical.

A LIGHT TO READ BY
Top: A poor light to read by in that it casts shadows in the wrong places.
Middle: You could provide a better light for the reader simply by extending the flex.
Bottom: The ideal solution is to have a light dedicated to the job. A narrow spot is preferable, but take care to balance the strength of the beam (its wattage) with the distance from the reader so that it is not overpowerful.

PLANNING AHEAD

The size of the sitting room and its layout dictate how many people can be seated and where the seating can be placed, and that in turn will determine where the light is needed. A light convenient to each and all is clearly the ideal solution; the number and position of wall sockets will be critical, so consider the lighting when planning the arrangement of the room.

LIGHTING TRACK
Above right: This scheme relies heavily on overhead lighting. The use of lighting track provides great flexibility and the well placed down-lighters make a strong, secondary focal point to balance the picture above the fireplace.

A GOOD MIX
Above left: This mixture of fixed and directional down-lighters, and a well placed up-lighter, achieves a good balance between the pools of light and shadow. The table light prevents the room from being too austere by adding a comfortable intimacy.

CONVENTIONAL SOURCES
Left: The strong feeling of comfort in this room is partly a result of the décor and furnishing and partly a result of the choice of luminaire. This form of lighting is ideal for this style of décor in that it appears intimate and cosy yet can still provide good practical light.

LOW-BUDGET CREATIVITY
Two simple multi-angle luminaires are all that is needed to give this sitting room a welcoming atmosphere, and are perfect to read by. A cleverly placed mirror enlarges the space without detracting from its sense of self-containment.

CREATIVE ADAPTATION

If you are working to a low budget, don't forget that the central pendant is really only a power outlet; one easy conversion is simply to lengthen its cable and hang it somewhere other than the middle of the room. With a long enough cable, the whole thing can be set at a much lower level and, with an appropriate shade, can suddenly become a much more pleasant feature.

LAMPSHADES

There is as wide a choice of lampshades as there is of luminaires, all of which will affect both the quantity and the quality of the light produced. The overall décor will affect your choice of lampshade, but always try to see them lit up before deciding, in order to judge the amount of light they are going to provide or how practical they will be. Of course, many shades are bought for their own decorative qualities, but do bear the overall scheme in mind when buying.

LIGHTING TRACK

Apart from the free-track systems discussed earlier, there are many fixed tracks and spot clusters on the market. They are mostly intended to replace the central pendant, but at that height, and since they are commonly limited to 60W lamps, they provide only very limited practical light. But they are useful for accent lighting, particularly for lighting pictures or throwing high-level light into corners.

MIXING IT

In a sitting room, a combination of directional down-light and scattered table lamps is most likely to prove the best solution. The choice depends on personal taste and budget – there are no obvious answers, but there are infinite possibilities and, once the practical needs are satisfied, you should set your imagination free, perhaps to include some special effects.

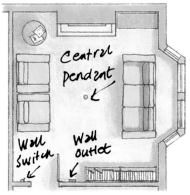

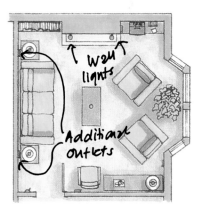

ORGANIZING THE WIRING
In many older sitting rooms you will find that the need for lighting and other electrical equipment has not been considered at all. With only the two electrical outlet sockets in the top diagram, your choices are limited largely to what you can do with the central pendant. It is difficult to provide good lighting without adequate electrical outlets. In the bottom diagram, the room has been provided with wall lighting and additional outlets for a more flexible lighting system. Don't forget that you will need power for your TV, Hi-Fi and so on; careful advance planning is essential.

NATURAL LIGHT

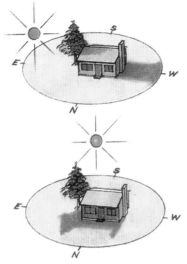

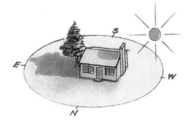

WINDOW SHADES

WHEN MOVING INTO A NEW HOUSE, YOU HAVE THE LUXURY OF CHOOSING WHICH ROOM TO MAKE YOUR SITTING ROOM, AND IT IS IMPORTANT TO BEAR IN MIND THAT MOST PEOPLE WILL ONLY USE IT DURING THE LATE AFTERNOON AND EVENINGS. CONSEQUENTLY, THE BEST ROOM TO USE, FROM THE POINT OF VIEW OF LIGHT, IS OFTEN ONE WHICH BENEFITS FROM THE AFTERNOON SUN AND PERHAPS THE SUNSET. EVEN IF YOU DON'T HAVE THE CHOICE, IT IS STILL IMPORTANT TO BEAR THE QUALITY OF THE NATURAL LIGHT IN MIND. A COLD NORTHERN LIGHT, FOR EXAMPLE, MAY DICTATE A WARM DÉCOR AND A SIMILAR LIGHTING SCHEME.

The colour of the curtains, just as the colour of the walls, will help to define the brightness of the room and its atmosphere. Very dark-coloured curtains tend to make the room feel smaller and more enclosed, whereas pale curtains will make the room feel larger and airier. If the sitting room is naturally dark, special light-enhancing net curtains are available. They tend to make the ambient light rather cold, but they do make the room feel a whole lot brighter, and a careful choice of lamps in the luminaires will counterbalance the coldness.

BLINDS
Right: The light from the fully glazed roof above this room has been softened by fitting roller blinds. This creates a diffuse light that could feel very cold were it not for the clever use of warm-yellow shades fitted to the table lights, which provide good reading light for the seating area, and cast warm tones on the walls and carpet.

CURTAINS
Far right: This room suffers from a low ceiling with dark beams, which would make it very dark and gloomy were it not for the light-coloured walls and the soft, pale coloured curtains, plus the two bright luminaires on the table.

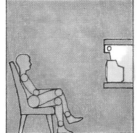

LIGHTING FOR THE TELEVISION

Lighting a room to accommodate a television is something rarely thought about, but bad lighting can seriously effect our enjoyment. The television often creates a strong focal point for the room, and thus will have a profound effect on its layout and lighting. If you are primarily a viewer, you will have less need for individual lighting than if you are primarily a reader, although the two are, of course, not mutually exclusive.

A television is itself a light source, but it is not a very strong one. Consequently it is easily overpowered by other sources, the most obvious being the sun. We are all aware of the advantage of placing the set with its back to the window, but we often forget that reflections will be created on the screen from artificial light in the room, and that the picture will be weakened by having a light too close to the side of a set. To many people, lighting for a television is not important, but it makes sense to consider it when planning your scheme.

The solution is simple: avoid strong lights behind the viewer or between the viewer and the screen. If you have a flexible system, you may even be able to design a particular set-up for watching television. Whatever system you employ, try to position the television set so that there is at least one good light behind it – enough to see by, but not enough to overwhelm the picture.

91

KITCHENS

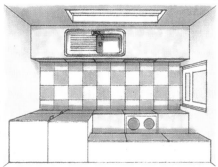

THE KITCHEN IS THE WORKSHOP OF THE HOME, AND THE BALANCE OF LIGHTING REQUIREMENTS MUST BE HEAVILY BIASED TOWARDS THE PRACTICAL. NOT ONLY IS IT A WORKING ENVIRONMENT, BUT THE NATURE OF THAT WORK REQUIRES A HIGH DEGREE OF FOCUS. BROADLY, THE KITCHEN CAN BE THOUGHT OF AS A GROUP OF INTERCONNECTED WORKSTATIONS FOR COOKING, SERVING, WASHING UP, AND SO ON, OFTEN WITH FOOD BEING PREPARED IN MORE THAN ONE PLACE. EACH TASK HAS ITS SPECIAL FACILITIES AND NEEDS ITS OWN LIGHT.

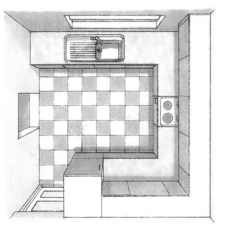

FUNCTION OR ATMOSPHERE

A GOOD SOLUTION
Opposite: This compact but well-arranged kitchen is ideally lit for the job. All the work surfaces are provided with good task lighting, which is supplemented by a down-lighter over the breakfast bar/servery.

The most common solution to the problem of lighting the kitchen is simply to install the largest fluorescent striplight possible within the space, and to do nothing else. This is a very easy and, in many ways, highly practical approach, but it leaves no possibility for atmosphere and can make a prolonged stint in the kitchen quite an unpleasant experience. The problem is that a fluorescent tube will bathe the room with a harsh, bland and shadow-free light, which can become very tiring.

Many people are returning to the use of natural materials in the kitchen, utilizing pine and oak finishes on cupboard doors, laying quarry-tile floors and introducing softer items like wicker baskets and pots of dried flowers. This sort of kitchen needs quite a different light from the fluorescent tube, but whether your taste runs to cottage-style or high-tech, well-planned task lighting makes the experience much more of a pleasure.

LAYOUTS

Most kitchens fall into one of three categories which, for the sake of clarity, can be called 'the galley', 'the standard' and 'the island'. But they will all have one thing in common – the bulk of the work surfaces are against a wall, and you will often be standing between your work and the available light.

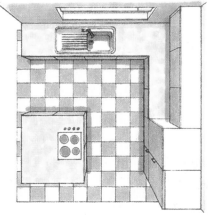

TYPICAL LAYOUTS
There are three main forms of kitchen layout, top: the galley, middle: the standard, and bottom: the island. Each of these arrangements presents particular problems for lighting, but the fundamental rule remains the same; for the preparation of food, good task lighting is a priority.

WORK SURFACES

Whether the preparation surfaces are continuous worktops, individual pieces of furniture, or simply a table, the light should not come from behind or directly above. Work-surface lighting is best if it comes from in front, or to one side, of the worker.

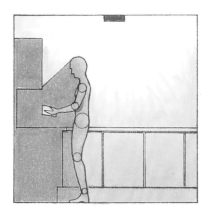

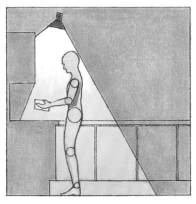

TASK LIGHTING
Good task lighting is that which illuminates the job without glare. Any light which casts shadows onto your work, as in the top diagram, is not good task lighting. The situation in the middle diagram is better, but you will need a lot of overhead spots to ensure you always have light coming from the side. The ideal solution, shown in the bottom diagram, is a concealed light source placed so that you cannot get in your own light.

ALTERNATIVES If you don't want to rewire your home, and there is a power socket available, crown-silver lamps in table lights are excellent for task lighting, in that they can be moved easily and provide strong light to the task without it shining in your eyes.

HOBS & COOKERS Lighting the cooker hob is no different or less important than the work surfaces, but is all too often forgotten. People with cooker hoods tend to rely on the built-in lights, but these are rarely effective because they are, of necessity, fitted with very low-wattage all-round-glow lamps, as low as 20W being common. The halogen spots with dichroic reflectors used in modern hoods are fine, giving a strong, clear, white light that is ideal for peering into steaming saucepans, but use enclosed lamps and remember to keep the glass clean.

KITCHEN SINKS It is common practice to site the kitchen sink under a window, and, during the day, the sink will often be the brightest point in the kitchen. This is merely tradition, and in these days of dish-washers and artificial light, it is hard to see why it persists. Direct lighting to the sink is less important than elsewhere, but some good light is useful at night, and the best answer is to treat the sink in the same way as the surfaces and the cooker.

OVERHEAD LIGHTING No domestic environment should rely on practical lighting alone; some accent light is necessary to provide an appropriate feel to the space. In the occasional need for atmosphere, the kitchen is little different from any other room and will benefit from a suitably shaded table light, or some down-lighting onto a table or breakfast bar. This is all the more important since many of us consult cookery books, at least occasionally, and need a good light to read by, away from the dirty or wet areas in the kitchen. Generally, a good first step would be to replace the fluorescent with a length of lighting track, but you will need to place the luminaires so that they can illuminate from an angle. You would be wise to include at least one down-lighter that can throw a pool of light into the centre of the room.

LIGHTING THE KITCHEN

Top left: This traditional kitchen uses a variety of light sources to achieve a good mix of task and accent lighting. The work surfaces and the cooker are supplied with dedicated task light, a length of track provides lighting to the shelving, and the central pendant throws a soft light overall. The period style of the luminaire blends well with the decorative scheme.

Top right: A modern kitchen, well lit for the job. Notice that the solution is very similar to the traditional kitchen; the task light is the same and down-lighters replace both the central pendant and lighting track. Note particularly that the two down-lighters on the left are directional, and are arranged so that the cupboard and the cooker are illuminated by overhead side light.

Bottom left: This island kitchen is less satisfactory in that the track is so placed that it would be difficult to avoid working in your own shadow.

Bottom right: These low-hung pendants make for a very atmospheric kitchen with just enough luminaires to avoid working in your own shadow. The cooker, however, is thrown into deep shadow by this arrangement, which might cause problems.

SHELVES & CUPBOARDS

If the kitchen has a walk-in cupboard or pantry, a fridge switch, operated by the action of opening or closing the door, is ideal, since the light is always on when you need it, but you cannot leave it on. Wall cupboards can usually borrow light from the task lighting, but if this is to be from luminaires mounted below the wall cupboards, a general wash of light at a higher level may be essential.

TABLES

If your kitchen includes space for a dining table, then the lighting needs to take account of it as a separate issue. This is dealt with in the following section.

DINING AREAS

MOST HOMES EITHER HAVE A LARGE KITCHEN OR LIVING ROOM WITH SPACE SET ASIDE FOR THE DINING TABLE, OR A SEPARATE ROOM IS DEDICATED TO EATING. IDEAS FOR LIGHTING APPLY EQUALLY WELL IN EITHER SITUATION, THE ONLY DIFFERENCE BEING THAT IT WOULD BE PREFERABLE IF THE LIGHTS COULD BE SWITCHED OFF IN THE KITCHEN AREA WHEN YOU ARE DINING. EITHER WAY, EATING IS A SOCIAL EVENT, AND A BADLY LIT TABLE CAN HAVE A PROFOUND EFFECT ON OUR ENJOYMENT.

GENERAL NEEDS

Lighting a dining room can be complex, because the space is used at different times of the day for meals needing quite different conditions. Broadly speaking, eating is no different from any other task in that it benefits from a good light dedicated to it. A light over the centre of the table is, without doubt, the most practical and effective way of providing illumination, and the most common form is a pendant. At a pinch, one light will do for all meals, but there are times when something special might be required, and that means flexibility.

BREAKFAST & LUNCH

Eating is curious, in that we feel quite differently about it depending on the time of day. Breakfast needs to be a fairly bright meal. It is a time when we prepare ourselves for the day, and a cheerful, sunny light is ideal. Even at the weekend, when you might linger over the newspapers, a good bright light is important. The meal at midday is rarely considered an occasion, and most people would be content with whatever light is available, artificial or natural. The evening meal, however, can be rather more demanding.

MIXED SOURCES
Opposite: A handsome billiard-table luminaire is the centrepiece of this dining room, and is supported by good natural light from the French windows and the accent illumination of the shelving behind.

MULTI-TASKING
Right: This magnificent billiard-table luminaire, controlled by a dimmer, serves admirably to illuminate the dining table, allowing for both a bright breakfast light and a softer, more subtle light for the evening.

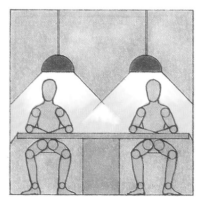

DINNER The word dinner can mean different things to different people; for the sake of clarity, this book will assume dinner to be the main meal of the day, usually eaten in the evening and sometimes as a form of social entertainment.

The candle-lit dinner – whether for two or a tableful – is famously attractive and atmospheric. Many households have special candle holders and, as discussed earlier, there is a wealth of candles available. Despite this, some find candlelight difficult to eat by and you may need to help it along.

Although it is rare in America, in the UK, a very common means of lighting the dining table is the 'rise-and-fall' pendant, which, if fitted with a dimmer switch, can be a very satisfactory solution. The rise-and-fall has its uses but it is a curious phenomenon. Once the light is set at a level whereby you can see well without being blinded, there should be no need to move it – which rather negates the need for it! Further, if you wish to move the table, perhaps for a party, then you are likely to want to move the light out of the way altogether, and very few people have a ceiling high enough. A better solution would be a light set at a fixed level, which can be removed entirely when not required. There are ceiling roses and luminaires that are designed specifically for this purpose. Not all dining tables are the same size, and some may require more than one light source to illuminate them satisfactorily. In these instances, you can install either a luminaire with more than one lamp holder, or a number of single luminaires, this latter being easier if you install a length of lighting track.

SERVING Where a dining room has a sideboard, it may be used for carving or as a servery. Both of these can be considered tasks, and good light is essential, particularly for carving. The sideboard is best lit in the same way as the kitchen work surfaces – avoid lighting that comes from behind or directly above. Make sure it comes from in front of you, or from one side. If you hold a lot of parties, a well-lit sideboard in the dining room is the ideal place to set out a buffet.

LIGHTING THE TABLE
Top: Any luminaire which leaves the lamp exposed to view should be avoided, but similarly, the luminaire should not be hung at such a level that diners cannot see each other. Middle: Fitting the luminaire with a deep shade would solve the problem but again, if it is hung at a fixed height, make sure you can see past it. Bottom: A very long table may need more than one luminaire; do not be afraid to fit as many as you need, either individually, or from a length of track.

LIGHTING FOR DINING

This sumptuous dining room results from the use of a subtle mix of light sources. The table itself has a strong central pendant, but with a deeply recessed and thus invisible lamp; the two overhead spots that light the picture, lift the room and prevent it from being too dark, and the side cabinets supply a rich warmth without diminishing the sparkle. The removal of any of these components would destroy what is in fact a fine balance.

CREATING THE MOOD People who use their dining room for entertaining will have a particular need to create a conducive mood, and the room will benefit from accent light in the same way as the sitting room. Track lighting can be particularly useful here, in that it can carry the pendant for the dining table as well as directional spots for illuminating pictures or features without extensive wiring or construction. The pendant can easily be moved or taken away altogether if necessary.

A combination of up- and down-lighting works well in the dining room, giving a concentrated light onto the table and a low level of background light to define the space without distracting the eye. It also provides a warm and inviting atmosphere. Low-wattage corner up-lighters from floor level can be particularly effective in dining rooms.

DESIGNING FOR ATMOSPHERE
Top: For many, the candle suggests romantic dining; but the more the merrier, as too few can be a problem. Six candles between eight people might not be enough for comfort.
Below: In contrast, this cheerful, sunny breakfast table takes full advantage of the orientation of the house but can still be used for a quiet, intimate supper.

MIXED LIGHTING FOR ATMOSPHERE
This charming dining room makes use of several dim lights, appropriately shaded, and uses the light from the window less for illumination than to provide a bright side light for daytime use. Notice that the central pendant is fitted with a rise-and-fall so that its height can be varied.

BEDROOMS

LIGHTING A BEDROOM IS INTERESTING SINCE, APART FROM ITS MAIN PURPOSE, IT SOMETIMES COMBINES THE FUNCTIONS OF BOTH THE SITTING ROOM AND BATHROOM. IT IS A ROOM WHICH MAY NEED FACILITIES FOR READING, IT MAY NEED FULL-LENGTH AND HEAD-AND-SHOULDERS MIRRORS LIT FOR PRACTICAL USE, AND IT MAY BE A PLACE TO KEEP SPECIAL PICTURES OR ORNAMENTS THAT WOULD BENEFIT FROM SYMPATHETIC LIGHTING.

READING

DESIGNING FOR REST
Opposite: A cool, calm and restful sleeping area. It would appear too cold but for the up-lighter beside the bed.

In the context of a bedroom, one usually reads in bed, and a bedside light is imperative. Even if you are not a reader, a bedside light is convenient, being the last thing you turn off at night and the first thing switched on in the morning. Reading in bed has its own problems, which can be alleviated by the right lighting. The table light at the bedside, powered from a wall socket, is probably the most common solution, but a wall light over the shoulder is ideal. In the case of double beds, two reading or bedside lights are best, so that one partner need not disturb the other. Do not forget the guest room; you may not be a bedtime reader, but your guests might be.

DRESSING TABLES

Apart from the bed, the dressing table is probably the most important area to light in a bedroom. As with the bathroom mirror, it is the face that needs to be seen clearly, and it is essential that the features are well-lit without glare.

Many people place the dressing table in front of the window, seeking to use natural daylight. But this is only relevant during the day, and often will obscure the light rather than exploit it, making the rest of the room gloomy. Lighting from both sides is ideal for a dressing table, and a pair of table lights in appropriate places is a simple solution which will not require any special wiring. Remember, two 60W lamps would be preferable to one 100W lamp, and will give you more light.

The same principles apply for full-length mirrors, but generally they will not need as much light as the dressing table, and it may be that ambient light is sufficient. Certainly, one good light from off-centre overhead will satisfy most needs.

DESIGNING FOR COMFORT
One well-placed bedside table with an interesting luminaire is, here, the complete answer for those more prosaic needs of a place to put the radio and perhaps a book or a glass of water. The luminaire is quite enough to read by, but is neither too bright nor intrusive.

WASHING EN SUITE
Far left: This wash basin is lit well for the purpose. The two side lights are ideal for shaving by since they cast light evenly to either side of the face and avoid the inevitable shadows cast by down-lighters.

THE DRESSING TABLE
Left: The same solution works equally well for a dressing table. In this case, luminaires are set at the appropriate height for a seated user.

BEDSIDE LIGHTING
Below left: An ideal situation for a double bedroom. The bedside lights are positioned so that each side is lit for reading. The switches are conveniently situated and neither partner need disturb the other.

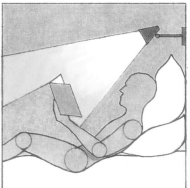

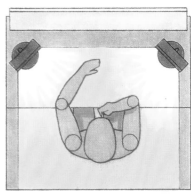

BEDROOM TASKS
Top: Ensure that the reading light is positioned either above or to one side or both, to avoid shadows being cast by your head.
Above: Similarly for a dressing table; the light should be placed so that the whole of the face is illuminated evenly.

CUPBOARD LAMPS
Low wattage, pygmy or pilot lamps, as used in refrigerators, are suitable for wardrobes and cupboards.

WARDROBES & CUPBOARDS

Depending on the room and other lighting, it is often useful to have a light in the wardrobe. This need only be a low-wattage lamp which can be controlled with a fridge switch in the same way as a kitchen cupboard or pantry. This would also provide for those with a full-length mirror mounted on the inside of the wardrobe door.

CREATIVE LIGHTING

The bedroom is private space. It offers the chance for fantasy and experiment – light it to suit! Any or all of the ideas outlined for sitting rooms would work equally well in the bedroom. Lighting from a track or a spot cluster could give light for the full-length mirror and any pictures you might have on the walls. Since the ceiling light is usually the one switched from the door, it makes sense to use it as creatively as possible.

WALL LIGHTS
A low-level wall light creates a pleasant atmosphere in this bedroom, with a style that goes well with the brass bed. Make sure you can reach the switch – nothing is more annoying than having to get out of bed to turn off the light.

COMFORT FOR KIDS

Left: The bedroom here shows the friendly approach one must consider when planning the lighting for young children.
Above: A humorous alternative for a child, providing light in an approachable and friendly way.

106

CHILDREN'S ROOMS

MANY PEOPLE WILL GO TO CONSIDERABLE LENGTHS TO DECORATE A CHILD'S BEDROOM IN A 'PLAYFUL' STYLE. OFTEN THE DÉCOR WILL FOLLOW A SPECIFIC THEME BASED ON THE CHILD'S INTERESTS, SOMETIMES WITH THE WHOLE ROOM BEING THOUGHT OF AS A PLAYTHING IN ITSELF. WHETHER OR NOT YOU CHOOSE TO GO TO THESE LENGTHS, A CHILD'S BEDROOM CAN PROVIDE GREAT OPPORTUNITIES FOR FUN LIGHTING, AND REMEMBER THAT THE CHILD WILL PROBABLY WANT TO HAVE A SAY IN BOTH THE DÉCOR AND THE LIGHTING AS HE OR SHE GROWS OLDER.

FUN LIGHTING

A ROOM FOR A CHILD
Right: In the top picture, the bunch of artificial tulips, each with a tiny lamp inside, makes an ideal luminaire for the situation. It serves no purpose but to brighten the fireplace and provide some fun. By way of contrast, the track lighting in the picture below is entirely practical. In this circumstance, track is excellent for providing flexible lighting well out of the way of young fingers.

Some of the ideas discussed for the sitting room can be equally effective in a child's bedroom. This is certainly a good place to introduce some animation, and while expensive projectors with gobo carriers are probably inappropriate for a child's room, remember that 'proper' luminaires are not the only way to achieve it. One form of animation not often considered is the flicker lamp – usually sold as substitute candles, these lamps give off no useful light but, with imagination, they can provide a fun source of accent light. Creating motion from the heat rising off a lamp is discussed on page 76, but, whatever special effects you do install, be certain to use non-flammable materials, and do not compromise the safety of the luminaire or, of course, the children.

DESK & STUDY LIGHTING

Children do a lot of reading as part of their studies, so make sure you provide enough of the right sort of light to avoid eye-strain. Consider this as another example of the home office (see pages 110–11), and remember that overhead light on a desk should be avoided, as it will inevitably create shadows on the work surface. A light that can be re-positioned to suit different short-term needs would be ideal, variations on the flexible-arm light being the most common; again, irrespective of the luminaire, make sure that it is clear, of the right strength and without glare. The addition of a table lamp dedicated to the desk can be used to enhance the overall lighting in the room.

LIGHTING FOR A YOUNG CHILD
Borrowed light from a door left ajar is ideal for very young children, since it also provides you with the chance to listen for any trouble. Dimmed overhead night lighting will continue to serve as part of a flexible scheme long after the child has grown beyond the need.

CHILDREN & COMPUTERS The child's bedroom is quite the most common place for the home computer. Whether it is used for games or serious study, the computer has become a significant part of children's lives, and they probably spend as much time in front of it as those adults whose work depends on the computer. The fact that a child's use often may be recreational makes no difference to the potential danger of prolonged exposure to the screen, even if the room is otherwise well lit. Try to encourage sensible practice (see also page 110) and remember that good lighting would keep the ambient light fairly subdued; keep the task light off the screen and set a comfortable balance between the brightness and the contrast of the screen output.

NIGHT LIGHTS Smaller children may need a dim light left on all through the night, and the conventional night light is found in many households. There are many specially made night lights, often of whimsical shape and design, and it should not be difficult to find one to suit any child. Night lights should give a soft, dim light, be cheap to run and use lamps with a long life span.

THE GROWING CHILD Children grow out of spaces like they grow out of clothes; their tastes will certainly change as they mature, and their need for practical light will become important. Older children will need more adult forms of lighting in addition to, or as a replacement for, the above, so it will pay to plan for the need at the outset. If you have the opportunity, provide as many wall sockets as you can for maximum flexibility; they can always be covered with blanking plates until they are wanted. You can also install some form of 'free' lighting track that can have luminaires added, taken away or just moved around as the need arises.

CHANGING NEEDS
A well-planned lighting scheme can provide your child with the correct light for changing needs while still satisfying the development of individual taste and ideas. It is particularly important that the lighting in a child's room does not cause eyestrain, contributing to eyesight problems for the future.

4 WORK SPACES

MORE AND MORE THESE DAYS, PEOPLE ARE EITHER WORKING FROM HOME OR ARE FINDING A NEED FOR SOME SORT OF PERSONAL OFFICE. THE WORK SPACE IS A PRIME EXAMPLE OF AN AREA WHICH NEEDS WELL-PLANNED TASK AND AMBIENT LIGHTING. NOTHING IS LESS CONDUCIVE TO WORK THAN AN UNCOMFORTABLE, POORLY LIT AND ILL-PLANNED ENVIRONMENT. HOWEVER, THERE IS NO REASON WHY YOUR HOME OFFICE SHOULD NOT BE AS COMFORTABLE AND PLEASANT AS YOUR SITTING ROOM.

HEALTH & SAFETY

In the commercial world, lighting is subject to extensive health-and-safety regulations, designed to reduce eyestrain for people at work. This is particularly important for computers users, who may have to spend many hours during a day looking at a screen. But for anybody whose work requires them to see fine detail clearly, to draw, or even just to read and write, eyestrain resulting from poor and ill-conceived lighting schemes is a very real danger – good lighting is therefore as essential to the home office as it is to the commercial workplace.

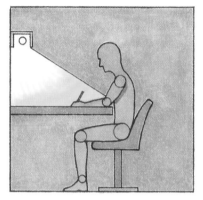

DESK LIGHTING

Very nearly every office or home workplace will have a desk, table or equivalent main working position, and the same rule applies here as it does in the kitchen: avoid lighting from above or behind, as this will inevitably create shadows on the work surface. Lighting from either or, preferably, both sides would be ideal, but any light that can be re-positioned to suit different short-term needs would suffice. Variations on the flexible-arm lamp are the most commonly available type of desk lighting. Everybody will have slightly different needs, but whatever lighting you decide upon should be clear, of the right strength and without glare. Try to provide a child's study area with the same balance that you would for your own, and encourage him or her to use it; in addition, provide sufficient accent lighting so that there is an acceptable level of ambient light.

TASK LIGHTING IN THE OFFICE
Top: Any lighting that casts shadows onto the work surface should be avoided or at best mitigated by some other source. Middle: A good solution is to provide a dedicated task light that illuminates clearly the work without light shining in your eyes. Bottom: The best solution is a combination. Good task lighting, well-balanced with general illumination from a pendant, will avoid much eyestrain.

LIGHTING THE COMPUTER
When using a home computer, make sure that you have a good task light that provides adequate illumination to the desk top and keyboard, but does not spill onto the screen.

COMPUTERS

Computers are a special case. They are becoming increasingly important to people who work from home, and, although much work has been done with screen technology to minimise eyestrain, there is still a very real danger if you do not take precautions. There are simple rules for computer operators, such as maximum lengths of time you should sit in front of a screen, but careful lighting will make a valuable contribution.

The computer is like a television in that it is a weak source of light, and it will be adversely affected by reflections and light spilling onto the screen. Conversely, the screen itself should not be over-bright. The best solution would be to maintain fairly subdued ambient light, while keeping the task light off the screen and setting a comfortable balance between the brightness and contrast of your screen output.

LIGHTING THE DESK
Below left: This modern home office has the optimum balance between accent light and task lighting. Neither would be sufficient on its own but together they create an ideal working environment.
Below right: A table light, assisted by a second luminaire to one side, provides balanced illumination to a traditional desk, without intruding upon the decorative scheme.

THE HOME STUDIO
Different work requires different lighting, and perhaps the best example is the artist's or designer's studio which has become synonymous with big north-facing windows. Anyone whose work requires them to see colour or fine detail will benefit from as much indirect, natural light as possible, though some artificial help is always useful.

GENERAL LIGHTING

If your work space is a desk in the corner of the sitting room or bedroom, or if you are obliged to work at the dining table, then the existing lighting may provide all the ambient light you need; provided the task lighting is adequate, you may already have an adequate solution.

Those with a room dedicated to their work will have more of a choice. People vary between those who like the office to be a strictly functional room and those who prefer a more intimate and relaxing environment. Either way, the lighting in a workroom should contribute to productivity by being both comfortable and efficient, and the techniques for general lighting are the same as those for a sitting room – interesting accent lighting balanced with sufficient task lighting to achieve the appropriate quantity and quality of ambient light. Even though it is a work space, many people like to create an intimate environment where they keep, not only the books and papers that are relevant to their work, but also pictures, objects and collections of personal interest. Such items provide an opportunity for some display lighting, being lit in the same way as those suggested for the hall or the sitting room, and this may be enough to provide necessary background lighting.

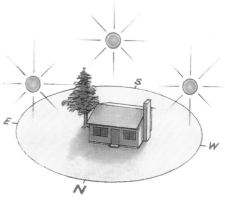

NORTH LIGHT
A cold northern light is ideal for matching colours. If you have the opportunity, choose a work room with big, north-facing windows.

DAYLIGHT & DAYLIGHT SIMULATION

For some, the nature of their work will be an important consideration. A reasonable amount of indirect, natural daylight has always been considered ideal illumination for any work that involves the recognition or matching of colours. Painting, designing, and even flower arranging are activities best undertaken in a north-facing room with a fairly large window.

Those without this choice or who have to work after dark should fit their task luminaires with daylight-simulation lamps. These are available in conventional lamp shapes with either ES or BC fittings, and also in fluorescent-tube form. The only drawback to the latter is that some people find the frequency of flicker inherent in fluorescent tubes to be disturbing, in which case they are best avoided. For most of us, however, this is not a problem, and the tube does have that special property of eliminating almost all shadow – a must for finely detailed work.

DAYLIGHT LAMPS
If you do not have the luxury of natural daylight, there is now a wide variety of lamps designed to simulate daylight.

BATHROOMS

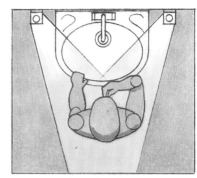

LIKE THE ENTRANCE HALL, THE BATHROOM IS ALL TOO OFTEN NEGLECTED WHEN IT COMES TO LIGHTING. THE SAFETY REQUIREMENTS IN AN ENVIRONMENT WHERE ELECTRICITY IS MIXED WITH MOISTURE ARE FUNDAMENTALLY IMPORTANT, BUT THIS DOES NOT MEAN THE BATHROOM HAS TO BE A PURELY UTILITARIAN SPACE, WITHOUT ANY FORM OF CREATIVE LIGHTING.

BATHROOM MIRRORS

LIT FOR MOOD
Opposite: In a well-appointed bathroom the use of multiple light sources results in a light level conducive to relaxation, but they are so placed that they also provide good task lighting for the washbasin and mirror.

There is only one item in a bathroom that requires good light – the mirror over the washbasin. Even in households with no men or none that shave, the mirror is where one needs the most light, and in many bathrooms this may be the only source of light. Lighting a mirror for practical use can be quite difficult. On the assumption that you need to see your own face, whether for shaving or applying make-up, it is essential that the light does not shine in your eyes. Ideally, it should illuminate the whole face, and not merely from one direction.

In theatre dressing rooms, mirrors are often lit from each side by a vertical row of lamps. Remember that six 20W lamps add up to 120W of light and will be very bright, so keep the numbers and the wattage down to a manageable level. A pair of globe carriage lights, intended to be set either side of the front door, can be a very effective way to light a mirror, and special mirrors with lighting built in are also available.

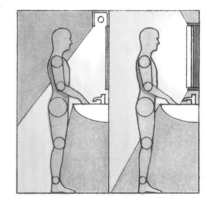

LIGHTING THE MIRROR
Top: A good solution. Strip lights are placed on either side of the mirror to throw shadow-free light onto the face.
Bottom left: Top light will do, but it is not ideal as it tends to throw shadow under the chin.
Bottom right: An illuminated mirror is perhaps ideal for this situation.

LIGHTING FOR MOOD

ATMOSPHERE BEFORE FUNCTION
Far right: The wall light in the bathroom, while satisfying admirably the requirements of the décor, is not ideal for practical purposes. Since there is but one light, half of the face would be thrown into deep shadow, making tasks such as shaving or applying make-up very difficult.

The bathroom is often somewhere we can relax, and good mood lighting should be given due consideration. Bathrooms don't need to be bright any more than they need to have high-gloss surfaces. Hygiene has nothing to do with glossiness, except in the mind. This is a preconception that we have grown out of in the kitchen – so why not in the bathroom?

From the point of view of creating the right mood, your bathroom is no different from your sitting room, and many of the ideas suggested for other living spaces are just as appropriate. Provided safety precautions appertaining to bathrooms are taken into account, down-lights, up-lights and other effects can all be put to good use.

BATHROOM LIGHTING
A single parabolic spot provides good illumination for those who like a long soak with a good book.

SPOT LIGHTING

For those who like to take a long soak with a good book, a strong, concentrated spotlight is a must in the bathroom. Simply replacing the original ceiling pendant with a single parabolic spot, and providing the mirror with two good side lights, is an excellent first step away from conventional utility bathroom lighting.

'WET LIGHTING'

MIRROR LIGHTING
Below: A pair of wall lights fixed at the optimum height provides the ideal solution for illuminating a mirror. Avoid using bright lamps, however – nothing more than 40W or you will dazzle the user.

There are many luminaires available that are specifically intended for use in wet places. The range is extensive, including versions of spotlights, floodlights, up- and down-lights and so on, and any luminaire designed for use in and around water can be used freely in a bathroom. Using these would enable you to build luminaires into the tiling of the bath or shower surround, and even into the floor if you do not use a standard shower tray.

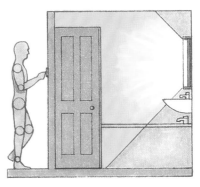

SAFETY

Whatever lighting you adopt for your bathroom, make sure you comply with the safety regulations. To avoid the risk of electric shock, bathroom lights are usually switched by means of a pull cord or from outside the room. Since this is sensible, if not compulsory, it is a good idea to plan a combination of practical and mood lighting that can be switched from a single point.

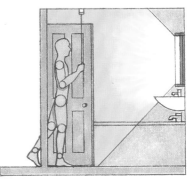

BATHROOM SAFETY
Above: In the UK, all lighting should be controlled either by a pull-string inside the bathroom, or a switch outside. In the USA this is not a problem, since ground-fault switches are the norm in 90% of installations.

A MIXED SCHEME
Left: This combination of theatrical dressing-table lights for the mirror and accent spotlighting, employed either for reading or simply for highlighting special features, makes for a very comfortable, well-lit bathroom.

ODD CORNERS

STORAGE SPACES ARE RARELY LIT ADEQUATELY, AND YET THERE ARE FEW PLACES IN THE HOME THAT WOULD BENEFIT MORE FROM DECENT ILLUMINATION.

ATTICS & LOFTS For many people, the roof-space is the main, and sometimes the only, space for storage. It is also where you are likely to find water tanks and other services, any of which might require maintenance or emergency attention, and yet home owners who have even installed loft ladders often neglect to provide suitable lighting. This, if anywhere, is the ideal place for a fluorescent tube. Its bright, diffuse light is perfect for eliminating shadow and enabling work to be carried out in even the most awkward corners. You would do well to fit as many as necessary, all switched from a central point adjacent to the hatch or door.

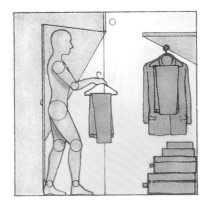

CUPBOARDS Walk-in cupboards are common enough to merit a mention, the traditional cupboard under the stairs being the most common. This is another place which too often becomes overfull and is difficult to see into. A combination of fluorescent light and fridge switches is ideal here, but make sure you do not use a fluorescent tube that needs a starter since the time delay, though short, will inevitably prove a nuisance.

LIGHTING ODD CORNERS
Top right: Shelves are best lit from above and to one side. Make the most of the available light by mounting the luminaire as far from the front of the shelves as possible. Middle right: Walk-in cupboards and wardrobes should be lit in much the same way, and perhaps fitted with an automatic switch. Bottom right: The loft would also benefit from an automatic switch, since it is all too easy to leave the light on once you have shut the hatch. However, a switch positioned near the top of the ladder or on a wall below would do equally well.

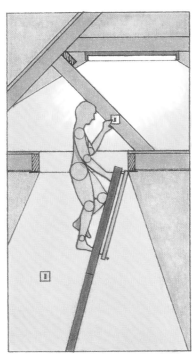

A CORNER KITCHEN
Even in a tiny kitchen tucked into a corner, there is no need for bad lighting. This little kitchen has been well provided with work-surface lighting, which also helps to illuminate the breakfast bar.

CHAPTER FIVE

LIGHTING OUTDOORS

WHETHER IN TOWN OR IN THE COUNTRY, A GARDEN IS USUALLY THOUGHT OF AS SOMETHING TO BE ENJOYED DURING MOMENTS OF RELAXATION; A PIECE OF PRIVATE LANDSCAPE TO BE SAVOURED WHEN SEEN FROM THE BEST ANGLES, PERHAPS USING SPECIAL VIEWING POINTS, ONE OR MORE OF WHICH MAY BE WITHIN THE HOUSE. HOWEVER, THE IDEA OF THE GARDEN AS A PICTURE IS A CONCEPT RESERVED LARGELY FOR THE HOURS OF DAYLIGHT. AFTER DARK, WE TEND TO IGNORE THE OUTSIDE AND, IN SO DOING, PASS UP THE OPPORTUNITY FOR A QUITE DIFFERENT, AND OFTEN MORE DRAMATIC, VIEW OF OUR GARDEN.

THE EXTRA ROOM

EVEN IN RELATIVELY MILD CLIMATES, SITTING IN THE GARDEN ON SUMMER DAYS IS TAKEN FOR GRANTED, AND THERE ARE MANY TIMES DURING THE YEAR WHEN IT IS POSSIBLE TO ENJOY THE GARDEN LATE INTO THE EVENING, SO IT IS HARDLY SURPRISING THAT THE EXPRESSION 'THE EXTRA ROOM' IS USED TO DESCRIBE THE BACK YARD AND GARDEN.

EXPLOITING POTENTIAL

Garden lighting is, at worst, considered to be a luxury that we can do without or, at best, exterior lighting is woefully limited and ill-considered.

Readers who enjoy cooking and eating outside, have probably installed lighting for that purpose, but how many of you have left the rest of the garden in darkness? This chapter is intended to enable you to take the ideas you have adopted for interior lighting out into the garden and exploit them fully.

PRACTICAL CONSIDERATIONS

There will be other practical considerations, such as lighting paths and driveways, but generally, garden lighting is something to have fun with, very much a theatrical affair. A good lighting scheme can transform the daylight scene, encourage practical night-time use, and still look attractive and exciting.

The garden can be large or small, hard or soft, modern or traditional; lighting works equally well. In gardens large enough to have walks and discrete areas, different moods and moments can be made, some which will entice you further and some which you will come upon suddenly, and with modern systems and fittings some quite startling effects are possible. Irrespective of the complexity of your garden layout, light can dramatize the best aspects and even create features of itself.

THE OPPORTUNITY
During the day, this charming patio, with its trompe l'oeil trellis, is cool and inviting and, with careful lighting, it could become a valuable extension of the room at night.

THE ROOM OUTSIDE
Opposite: The combination of glass and light makes this garden almost at one with the kitchen. It feels like a single space, inviting one in from the garden or out from the house, and fully exploits the garden's potential for enjoyment after dark.

5 POWER OUTDOORS

THE CHOICE OF A MAINS- OR LOW-VOLTAGE SYSTEM IS FUNDAMENTAL TO ANY GARDEN-LIGHTING PROJECT. YOUR CHOICE WILL BE INFLUENCED BY WHAT LUMINAIRES ARE AVAILABLE LOCALLY AND HOW MUCH YOU WANT TO SPEND, BUT IT CAN HAVE A FAR-REACHING EFFECT ON WHAT CAN BE ACHIEVED. THIS IS ONE DECISION THAT WILL HAVE TO BE TAKEN AT THE VERY EARLIEST STAGE OF PLANNING AN EXTENSIVE GARDEN-LIGHTING INSTALLATION, SINCE IT MAY INVOLVE CONSIDERABLE WORK AND WILL BE DIFFICULT TO REVERSE LATER.

MAINS VOLTAGE Installing an electrical circuit outdoors introduces a wholly different set of rules. Mains voltage has the advantage that all the equipment and materials will be tried-and-tested, and will be readily available, but an exterior system will involve power cables of the correct rating, possibly in conduit and certainly so if it is to be buried. The luminaires and junctions will need to be waterproof, and it may be necessary to install a subsidiary distribution board if you have a large garden.

All this will be considerably more expensive to purchase than an interior system, and will almost certainly require professional installation to be sure of safety. A mains-voltage system should be considered if the project is likely to include taking power out into the garden, to run water pumps or electric cooking facilities, for example, but if not, there is really no need to go to these lengths now that low voltage is becoming so much more readily available.

LOW VOLTAGE In places where there is good range of luminaires on the market, low voltage is a very attractive alternative. It may still appear to be expensive to install, since it will require stepped-down power, but the savings in other areas should more than compensate for the initial cost of the luminaires and transformers. This may be one large transformer, groups of smaller ones, or transformers integral to each luminaire. The choice is largely dependent on the size of the project and is fairly easy to calculate; for example, one 100W capacity transformer can run 2 x 50W or

60W TRANSFORMER

100W TRANSFORMER

TRANSFORMERS
Transformers can take a variety of forms, these being typical shapes and ratings. The top one is rated at 60W, which means you can run, for example, three 20W luminaires or two at 30W. The bottom one rated at 100W, allows you a bit more flexibility, and is worth considering even if you don't need to use its full capacity for the time being.

A TYPICAL OUTDOOR-LIGHTING SET
If your circumstances allow, these pre-wired sets are very easy to install and use. Three discreet down spot-lights might be all you need around a small pool, for instance, or to illuminate a pathway.

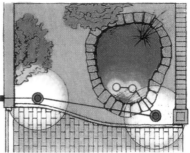

ONE LARGE TRANSFORMER

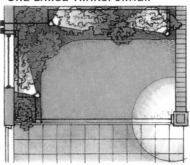

GROUPS OF SMALLER ONES

5 x 20W lights. Once installed, the advantages are many: the luminaires are smaller and can be much more discreet, the lamps have a longer life span and are cheaper to run, and the cable can be lightweight, needing no special safety precautions. There are a number of low-voltage outdoor-lighting sets available, most of which use some form of clip-in cable which enables the user to connect or disconnect a luminaire at will, without any fiddly wiring.

COMBINING BOTH SYSTEMS

In larger gardens, a sensible solution might be to run mains voltage to a number of selected distribution points and then run low-voltage sub-systems from them. One advantage might be that mains power would then be available in remote parts of the garden, for such things as water pumps or for providing light and heat to a garden house or a swimming pool.

In the garden, we are even more concerned with the creation of atmosphere than we are inside the house. Gardens can be both mysterious and exciting, particularly at night, and any lighting scheme should seek to exploit this. There is no point to the exercise if all we are going to do is floodlight the place as if it were a car park.

And remember the golden rule: if possible, no light source should ever be visible directly.

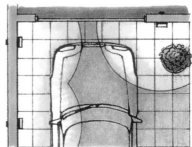

INTEGRAL TRANSFORMER

ALTERNATIVE CIRCUITS
Three examples of alternative wiring set-ups. The top one has one large transformer running a number of luminaires. The middle picture shows two smaller transformers, an arrangement which allows greater flexibility, and the bottom installation uses luminaires with integral transformers.

EFFECTS & IDEAS

THE LIGHT SOURCES DESIGNED FOR EXTERIOR LIGHTING ARE MUCH THE SAME AS THOSE USED INSIDE THE HOUSE, IRRESPECTIVE OF VOLTAGE LEVEL AND THE EFFECTS YOU WANT TO CREATE. THE MAIN DIFFERENCES BETWEEN LIGHTING A GARDEN AND LIGHTING A HOUSE ARE THAT THE EMPHASIS IN THE GARDEN WILL BE MUCH MORE ON ACCENT LIGHTING THAN ON PRACTICAL, AND THERE WILL RARELY BE A CEILING TO HANG LIGHTS FROM!

UP-LIGHTING

Up-lighting can be used on a grand or an intimate scale. A wide floodlamp set at ground level is excellent for illuminating a large feature tree or the façade of your house, but floodlighting, commonly used for the illumination of public buildings, is just that – a saturation of light. Spotlighting is much better for picking out detail or highlighting features by means of strong light/shade contrast.

By comparison, small ground-level or sunken up-lighters, placed beneath shrubs or small trees, or among groups of containers, can produce very interesting and intimate effects, and can define the shape of the garden without exposing all its secrets at once.

DOWN-LIGHTING

The situations where down-lighters are used most often are in pergolas and covered walks, or on balconies and patios, customarily at shoulder height or above. They are also employed to light garden paths and driveways, but set much closer to ground level.

High-level down-lighting is rarer and more difficult to get right, and should only be used in moderation. As an effect, it is best used among trees to introduce a suggestion of moonlight, but since it is possible to make too much of the effect, ensure it is appropriate for your circumstances. Remember, you are not floodlighting a sports stadium. If you do want to suggest moonlight, it is not necessary for the light to be very bright, but it must be towards the blue end of the spectrum, and the correct choice of lamp or filter is critical.

UP & DOWN
Opposite: The value of mixing light sources can be seen clearly in this small yard. The down-lighters on each side pick out specimen plants and planters, and illuminate the path, while the up-lighter on the balcony increases the scale of the space and adds a touch of grandeur.

UP-LIGHTING
A small formal fountain like this is a good candidate for up-lighting. Scale makes little difference: whether it is a fountain, a tree, or a house, the same principles apply.

COLOURED LAMPS
The choice of lamps is limited to a few primary colours such as red, green, yellow and blue. Greater subtlety can be achieved using filters, but they may not be easy to fit to your luminaires. Some pre-wired kits come with built-in coloured filters, but they are limited generally to the same primary colours.

COLOUR & TONE

The colour of the light is just as important outside as in. At night the only natural light is from the moon and stars, both of which give a cold light at the blue end of the spectrum, and any other colour cannot but look artificial. Used intentionally, coloured light is fine – for example, to highlight and enhance the natural colours of a feature – but indiscriminate use of coloured lamps can be disastrous unless you want your garden to look like a fairground.

The best way to handle colour in the garden is to keep it very simple. If a contrast is sought, keep it subtle – simply fitting a conventional filament lamp next to a halogen lamp will give you a contrast without overstatement. Remember, it's not generally the lighting you want to see, but that which is lit by it.

COLOUR
This design by John Vellam incorporates a dramatic use of strong colours. This is lighting as a feature in itself rather than illumination for the garden. Like any creative activity, lighting of this sort needs to be handled with expert care if it is to be successful without overpowering the garden itself.

COLOURED LAMPS
& FILTERS

There are two ways to introduce stronger colour, either with coloured lamps or with coloured filters or 'gels'. The range of coloured lamps for exterior situations may be limited to one, often strong, shade of red, blue, yellow or green, and subtlety will be very difficult to achieve. The colours available in gel are, however, very much more extensive, ranging from the intense to the faintest tint, allowing tight control of effects. You can acquire coloured gel from theatrical-supply stores, and make sure you do use the proper material, as it is heatproof and designed for the purpose. Unfortunately, very few luminaires for the domestic market will have gel holders, so it may be necessary to invent your own. If you going to try making your own, be sure to use only heatproof materials throughout, and do not compromise the integrity or safety of the luminaire.

SPECIALS Lights strings with coloured lamps are often erected temporarily for parties and other celebrations, but if used outside on a mains-voltage system, they should always be run through a contact breaker or preferably wired as a permanent installation, in which case endeavour to keep their switching independent of any other garden lighting, since they tend to suggest a party atmosphere which may not always be appropriate. Greater flexibility is possible using low-voltage systems, and strings of lights add random sparkle within shrubs or trees, and can be very effective when hung at a low level. In these circumstances, white lamps would be a wiser choice than coloured ones, and there is no need to reserve effects like these for Christmas.

AVOIDING GLARE
Above: The level of ambient light in a garden will be lower than indoors and, consequently, it is even more important to place your luminaires carefully to avoid glare.

DRAMATIC SHADOWS
Right: Dramatic shadows are cast by a powerful up-lighter shining through the foliage of this magnificent specimen tree. The shrub's silhouette is softened by a side light to the right, and the whole scene is back-lit by a second up-lighter under the pergola.

GARDEN FEATURES

A GARDEN IS OFTEN CREATED AS A SERIES OF SET PIECES THAT FALL WITHIN TWO CATEGORIES – THOSE WHICH ARE DESIGNED AS FOCAL POINTS, AND THOSE WHICH ARE INTENDED AS VIEWING POINTS FROM WHICH TO ADMIRE THE FORMER. THEY ARE NOT MUTUALLY EXCLUSIVE, OF COURSE; MANY OF THEM MAY BE BOTH. JUST AS WE BEGUN INDOORS BY LISTING ACTIVITIES AND TASKS, A GOOD START OUTDOORS IS TO ANALYZE THE GARDEN TO ESTABLISH HOW BEST TO LIGHT THOSE AREAS WHERE YOU WILL BE SITTING, THE VIEWING POINTS, AND THOSE THAT ARE TO BE SEEN FROM SOME DISTANCE.

DEFINING FEATURES
A strong spot down-lighter, trained on the centre of this group of planters, holds the group together and defines the trellis with shadow.

CHANGING SCALE

With the right lighting, it is possible to alter visually the whole scale of the garden, even to invent features that are not really there. It is not even necessary for there to be a real path or steps for example – the whole layout of the garden can be altered in the imagination by the careful use of light.

DECKS & PATIOS

A deck or patio often becomes a sort of outdoor sitting room, and they are the most likely places to sit outside at night. The lighting should be more for effect than practical, and it is important to bear in mind that too much light tends to eclipse the lighting in the rest of the garden. A good solution would be to have some low-level down-lighting, perhaps under benching or among planters, placed so that it throws shadow upwards and does not shine light into your eyes. If the space is to double as an eating area, one or more narrow-beam, shielded down-lighters would provide light without obscuring the view, particularly if they were switched separately.

A PATIO SITTING ROOM
Very much an outdoor sitting room, this patio is lit by feature up-lighters which provide soft pools of light, causing the shrubs to glow like lanterns. Notice that the garden statue is lit from the side to emphasize the modelling.

PATHS, STEPS & DRIVEWAYS

Lighting for garden walkways is designed partly for safety but also to draw the eye in a chosen direction after dark in the same way as the path itself does during the day. Ideal for path lighting are low-level shaded luminaires, with under-step strips, and illuminated bollards for the driveway. If a path is laid without hazardous changes of level, string-lighting may be less obtrusive and serve equally well. For safety, it is wise to provide some path lighting around the edge of a swimming pool or garden pond.

PERGOLAS A pergola should be treated in some respects like a path, and can be lit similarly. There may be places where down-lighting can be employed to emphasize a special feature beneath a pergola, or perhaps to illuminate a garden bench or seat, but too much light tends to make a pergola feel like an enclosed space, so use it with care.

TREES & SHRUBS It is as easy to over-light a garden as it is a house, and with the same result – there's no atmosphere. In an informal setting, it is probably the trees and shrubs that define the garden's shape and form. This is no less true at night, the only difference being that shape and form will be defined by darkness rather than light, that is by the shadows that are cast.

Here is a rule of thumb for lighting large, dense objects. A light placed behind a shrub tends to throw it into silhouette, giving it size without form, while a similar light placed in front has the reverse effect. Clearly then, a combination of back lighting and front lighting will achieve the best result. By defining the tree, the light also defines the space it occupies.

Trees and shrubs are best lit from below and, if you have the space, with the luminaire hidden behind a smaller shrub planted between the subject and the viewer. Keep the light sympathetic – try using a lamp or gel that will enhance a tree's natural colour. Yellow light will bring out the greenness of deciduous foliage and grass in a way that green light will not, and blue light might be a better choice for coniferous trees.

STATUARY & SCULPTURE Not all statuary is grand – even a modest garden gnome, can form a focal point – and it is certain to be improved by illumination. Depending on the piece, light will help define it and give it shape. Conversely, a badly placed light may distort its shape, and positioning, intensity and focus must be given due attention. Once again, low-level lighting set at an oblique angle is a good starting point, but experiment before deciding on the final position. If possible, try consulting the artist about appropriate lighting for a piece of sculpture – he or she may have strong opinions!

TREES & SHRUBS
A single well-placed floodlight illuminates this tree and garden seat, creating one cohesive feature. The lamp throws a warm yellow light that provides emphasis without bleaching out the natural colours.

ARBOURS & GAZEBOS

These are the features which may well need lighting, both as viewing points and as objects to be admired. Low-level up-lights, from concealed sources, would suit the exterior, with a single narrow spot creating a contrasting central pool of light on the inside. Take care that any lighting does not obscure your view from the arbour or gazebo.

A garden feature of this sort may be placed to look out beyond the garden, a view which may be worth considering as part of your scheme. Combining the visual effects within your garden with light sources outside the boundaries can extend the perceived threshold into infinity. This same principle is adopted by the designers of Japanese gardens, who use the 'landscape without' to focus and frame the 'landscape within'.

LAWNS

Direct light onto a lawn is generally of little use unless the intention is to provide light for a specific activity. Oblique light is a more satisfactory solution for lawns lit for atmospheric effect. Borrowed light from other features may be sufficient to illuminate a lawn, though one or more spotlights set at ground level will emphasise the topography and help define or create shape and form.

Lighting a patch of grass or lawn that is partially obscured from view can be particularly successful. A half-hidden pool of light can make a garden seem larger than it is in reality, enticing the viewer to explore.

LIGHTING TREES
A light placed behind a dense tree or shrub throws it into silhouette, emphasizing shape and size only. If lit from the front and below, the tree has form but no indication of size. With two up-lighters, the whole character of the tree is revealed.

WATER FEATURES

WATER IN A GARDEN REQUIRES SPECIAL ATTENTION. IT MAY BE A LAKE, IT MAY BE A STREAM OR EVEN A RIVER, IT MAY BE A WATERFALL, OR PERHAPS NO MORE THAN A SMALL FISH POND WITH A FOUNTAIN. SIZE, WHEN IT COMES TO WATER FEATURES, MAKES LITTLE DIFFERENCE; THE PRINCIPLES ARE THE SAME, HOWEVER, WHATEVER THE SCALE. REMEMBER THAT ALL OUTDOOR LIGHTS AND ELECTRICAL FITTINGS SHOULD BE WATERPROOF AND BE SURE TO SEEK ADVICE ON LOCAL SAFETY STANDARDS.

STATIC OR FLOWING?

Water can take two forms, static or flowing, and either can produce stunning effects when appropriately lit. If it is moved by artificial means, there will be times when the water is still, as when the flow pumps are turned off. There will also be times when the water will be in motion, perhaps ruffled by a breeze. Anyone lighting water would be wise to bear these two facts in mind, as they can be turned to advantage.

ABOVE THE SURFACE

All above-surface lighting involves reflection, and an illuminated feature seen from across a stretch of water is one of the most evocative of sights. Known also as mirror-lighting, the technique can be used on even the most modestly sized pond. More than likely you won't have a lake with a Greek temple set romantically on the far shore, but you may have a particularly attractive planter or jardinière, or perhaps a piece of sculpture, any of which will make an ideal subject for mirror-lighting. Even when the surface of the water is moving, the reflections will still look attractive.

WATER AS A MIRROR
Light spilling from the doorway, combined with lights strung along the pool steps, produce a dramatic scene that amply demonstrates the effects of mirror lighting.

MOTION & ANIMATION

Shining a spotlight onto a stream from a low angle bounces light off the running water onto whatever happens to be in its way, a rock for example, painting its surface with a rippling, ever-changing pattern that can be a very exciting visual effect. 'Borrowed' motion of this sort is a good way to introduce animation into a garden, since it does not require special luminaires, and surface lighting is a much more satisfactory technique for a natural stream than submerged lighting.

THE SWIMMING POOL
This pool is illuminated with submerged wall lights that provide an exciting glow while providing adequate practical light for safety.

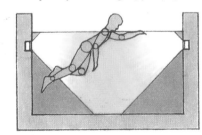

ACCIDENTAL LIGHT

Whether the setting is formal or informal, water benefits from illumination, but the light need not be integral with the water.

In the formal pool, left, the lights from the cloister are reflected in the still water, which acts like a perfect mirror. In the natural pool, below left, the abundant water plants create a quite different effect. In this case, submerged lighting would be quite inappropriate.

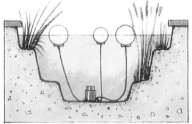

FEATURE LUMINAIRES

These special globe lights float on the surface of the water, and are powered from a transformer placed on the bottom of the pool. Feature luminaires like these can be used in any pool of the appropriate depth.

FOUNTAINS

An up-lit fountain is one of the most striking effects you can create. The lamps need to be at least 100W in order to compensate for the density of the water. Many of the luminaires made for use underwater are provided with filter holders, so it is relatively simple to add colour.

LIGHT FOR ITS OWN SAKE

Water features provide an excellent opportunity for using light for its own sake, and are perfect for special effects using lasers or projections. However, specials of this sort should be used with caution, not least because they are likely to be very expensive. Bear in mind also that you are lighting the garden, not creating a theme park.

UNDERWATER

Submerged light is most useful when the water feature is obviously artificial. In cases where a pool is a formal shape with hard edging, underwater lighting can have great impact, but where a water feature is intended to appear natural, or really is natural, submerged lights only serve to destroy the illusion. This may be your intention, but if not, avoid underwater lighting altogether. Light shining up through the surface of a pool will move with the water, throwing moving shadow and light onto an overhanging rock or shrub.

One good place to put a submerged spotlight is below a fountain or positioned so that it serves as an up-light for a waterfall. This sort of lighting makes a dramatic focal point of any water feature, but it is more appropriate in a formal design.

BRIDGES

As any visitor to cities like Paris or Prague will testify, bridges are superb when illuminated. It is not likely that lighting the superstructure would be appropriate in a garden setting, where the overall effect is likely to be more subdued, but up-lighting the underside of a bridge can produce very dramatic effects. Even on a modest scale, this is worth considering if you have a bridge/water combination that can be seen from a distance.

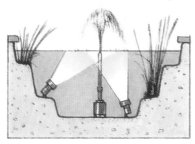

WATERPROOF LUMINAIRES

Be sure to install only luminaires made specifically for use underwater. Never experiment and be sure to follow the manufacturer's instructions carefully. Many luminaires use the water as a coolant and they should not be switched on until they are submerged.

135

EATING OUT

ENTERTAINING OUTDOORS IS VERY POPULAR, EVEN IN TEMPERATE CLIMATES, AND IT IS A MUST IN MANY PLACES, PARTICULARLY DURING THE EVENING. A WELL-LIT AREA FOR COOKING AND EATING IS ESSENTIAL, BUT REMEMBER, 'WELL-LIT' IS NOT SYNONYMOUS WITH 'BRIGHTLY LIT'; THERE IS NO NEED FOR THE LIGHTING IN THESE AREAS TO ECLIPSE THE REST OF THE GARDEN.

COOKING

For cooking outdoors, the same rules apply as in the kitchen. The light should come from in front or from the side, and should project downwards into pans or onto the grill surface. It should illuminate the adjacent surfaces where food is to be prepared or is being served, and it should not spill beyond the cooking/serving surface any more than necessary, or it may interfere with lighting installed elsewhere in the garden.

EATING OUT
Opposite: An intimate dining table in the garden. The concealed up-lighters around the perimeter of the garden give a pleasant, ambient glow, while the lantern on the table provides excellent light to eat by.

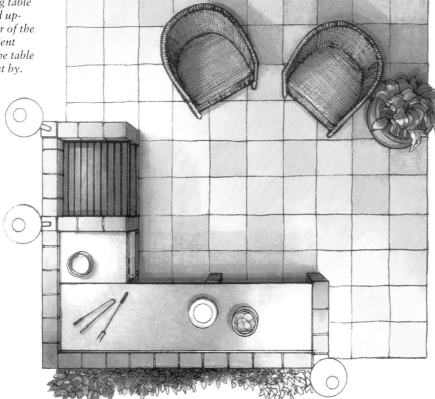

COOKING OUTSIDE
Left: the three pathlighters mounted on top of the wall behind the barbecue and preparation surfaces make an ideal area for cooking and eating. A less happy arrangement is shown in the picture above. The wall light provides adequate overall illumination, but the cooking area itself is poorly lit, with a deep shadow cast onto the barbecue itself.

137

EATING OUTSIDE

A pergola provides an ideal solution to lighting an outdoor eating area. Narrow spot down-lighters, mounted to the beams above, can be focused directly onto the table, minimizing light spill that might eclipse subtle garden lighting elsewhere.

A SINGLE LIGHT SOURCE

A single down-lighter set directly above the table amply illuminates the author's own outdoor eating area, yet still allows other, distant lights to be appreciated. Carefully placed garden candles provide additional atmosphere.

An eating area in the garden is just a dining room alfresco, and many of the ideas suggested elsewhere for dining rooms will be of equal importance outdoors. Many people who regularly cook outside, whether at night or during the day, fail to provide somewhere to eat in comfort, often relying on the strategic use of laps and other handy surfaces. Apart from the inconvenience this causes, it is impossible to provide adequate lighting in such an ad hoc situation, resulting in an experience which is anything but pleasurable.

One of the best locations for eating outdoors, and certainly from the point of view of lighting, is a garden pergola. It provides the necessary ceiling for installing down-lighting, and it can be lit in very much the same way as an indoor dining room, with one central light and peripheral up-lighters at ground level or under benching. Where a pergola is inappropriate, carefully positioned pathlighters can provide side-light to eat by, as well as local lighting for a patio.

Entertaining does not necessarily include eating, of course, and lighting a patio or paved area adjacent to the house is a useful way of providing overspill space for larger parties, when the extra room becomes vital.

Do not forget the general plan, and make sure the lighting is integrated with the rest of the garden. If the eating and cooking area is a separate unit, you may want to control its lighting independently from the other garden lighting.

MULTIPLE LIGHT SOURCES
*In this garden, designed by the
author, the half pergola lit from
above, borrows light from the
ground-level up-lighter above the
waterfall and the outdoor candle on
the deck. With very little visible light
beyond the garden, this makes for a
very intimate corner.*

A GLOW IN THE GARDEN
*For less temperate climates and during the winter, the
garden can still be considered part of the house for sitting
or eating. A conservatory lined with plants, and with the
right balance of light, has the effect of dissolving the
barrier between inside and out, even at night, and looks
spectacular from outside.*

139

GARDEN ROOMS

A WELL-CONSIDERED CONSERVATORY CAN HAVE THE EFFECT OF
BLURRING THE BOUNDARY BETWEEN THE INSIDE OF THE HOUSE AND
THE OUTSIDE, BRINGING THE GARDEN INTO YOUR HOME OR,
CONVERSELY, EXTENDING THE INTERIOR OUT INTO THE GARDEN. IN
DAYLIGHT, THIS IS COMPARATIVELY EASY — A WELL-DESIGNED
PLANTING SCHEME ALONE CAN ACHIEVE THIS — BUT AT NIGHT THE
EFFECT IS EASILY LOST.

THE CONSERVATORY AS A SITTING ROOM

Whether you have a garden room with large sliding patio
doors or French windows, or a fully glazed conservatory that
actually obtrudes into the garden, lighting these spaces is
similar to lighting a sitting room, with the balance perhaps
more on accent than practical lighting. However, it is important
to bear in mind that any lighting indoors tends to turn the
windows into mirrors, and will to some extent eclipse the
lighting outside. A good solution would be to have low-level
down-lighting inside, perhaps under benching or among
planters, placed so that it throws shadow, rather than light,
onto the glass. In this way, any lighting in the garden will be
visible from inside, and should more light be needed, narrow,
shielded down-lighters would act in much the same way. If you
are unsure of the best way to achieve the required effect, it
might be worth obtaining a few clip-on spots with trailing
leads and experiment by moving them around until you reach
the best compromise before committing yourself to a
permanent installation.

THE GLASS WALL
*Opposite: Full-length glazing
minimizes the barrier between the
house and the garden. Blinds will
provide privacy when its needed, but
they are not so dense as to cut the
outside off entirely. With well-
balanced lighting, this patio garden
can be enjoyed equally well at night
as during the day.*

THE TRADITIONAL CONSERVATORY

If the conservatory is used for its traditional purpose of
growing plants from tropical or semi-tropical climates, it is
likely to contain a fairly high level of moisture, and it may be
necessary to use waterproof luminaires. If you are in any doubt,
you should consult a specialist. The traditional conservatory is
one of the few places where fluorescent lighting can prove really
useful, in the form of the 'Gro-Lux', a special plant-growth-
enhancing tube that is available from specialist lighting retailers
or garden centres.

BORROWED LIGHT
*The wealth of glass and a careful
mix of light sources, both inside and
out, achieve a fine balance which
brings the whole group together as
one space. By borrowing some light
from the outside, the glazing
becomes less obtrusive and the
garden becomes an integral part of
the house.*

DISSOLVING THE GLASS
A concealed strip light below the window sill, combined with strong up-lighters in the garden outside, has the effect of removing the glass altogether. If you want reading light, take care to screen its reflection with a tall plant group, for example.

THE GARDEN ROOM

Like a conservatory, a garden room – that is, a room with French windows or patio doors – can be made to capitalize on its relationship with the garden at night as much as during the day. The effect will be different to that described earlier, but it need not be any less attractive.

BRINGING THE GARDEN INDOORS
A careful balance of up-lighters on either side of the glass, as shown below, brings the garden into the house by effectively removing the glass. Be sure to keep outdoor lights brighter than those indoors, and make sure little or no light spills onto the glass itself.

CONSERVATORY OR PERGOLA
The conservatory left is lit both from inside and out. It borrows light from a house window and the patio behind, so that you are hardly aware that it is glazed at all; the structure becomes more like a pergola than a conservatory.

142

Place some discreet up-lighters among pots and shrubs just outside the glass, and some slightly dimmer ones among grouped house plants on the inside. If done carefully, this makes the glass appear to vanish. Of course, any garden room may still be used for practical purposes, and if reading light, for example, is required, keep it very subdued and local to where it will be used. This technique is particularly effective when the whole garden is lit with the view from the garden room or conservatory in mind.

THE GARDEN HOUSE

An open-air structure, such as a gazebo or an arbour, can be lit very easily as described above, but the moment you introduce glass you create a problem. As is the case with conservatories, any glass will become a mirror if the position and balance of the light are not carefully controlled. If it is intended to use a summer house or similar at night, the same rules apply and the same solutions can work equally well. Keep the light at or near ground level, and shield any light sources so that no light shines directly onto the glass.

AN INTEGRATED GROUP

The same structure seen from both inside and out (above left and right). From inside, the minimal garden lighting turns the windows into mirrors, reflecting the candles and the table lamp, making the whole space feel large and airy. From outside, however, the effect is quite different. The seating area on the patio, while taking some light from the bulkhead luminaire over the door, borrows, not just the light, but the whole atmosphere of the conservatory and sitting room, and that, combined with the white-painted section of wall, brings the whole area together. With all the doors open, you might move from one space to another, scarcely aware that you had passed outside.

5 **OUTDOORS** GARAGES & PATHWAYS

As with cupboards and storerooms within the house, the paths and, to a lesser extent, the garage are all too often neglected. The size and relative importance of the task depends on the scale of the garden – a large garden is likely to have one or more outbuildings already supplied with light and power. But whatever the scale, most people would benefit from light to and in the outbuildings.

SHEDS   Fluorescent light really comes into its own for outbuildings. The shed is a working utilitarian space that really benefits from the bright, diffuse light that a fluorescent lamp provides. However, although the diffuse nature of fluorescent light gives an even spread, it doesn't eliminate shadows entirely – if it is used to illuminate a work surface, the luminaire should be placed so that you do not come between it and your work. This is the same principle as that used in the kitchen, but it is rarely applied in such a humble environment as the shed.

GARAGES   Unless the garage is also used as a workshop, its only lighting requirement is to access the car. Since one has to enter and leave the garage in the car, it is a good idea to have some sort of automatic or semi-automatic lighting. This is another ideal place for one or more heat- or motion-triggered lights. These should be placed so that they are activated on approach, either in the car or on foot, and so that they illuminate the space, both inside and out.

INDIRECT PATH LIGHTING
Small, elegant up-lighters directly illuminate the flowers, whilst providing indirect light to the patio.

AUTOMATIC LIGHTING
A light, or group of lights, can be fitted with motion-detecting switches operated by the car or by the driver approaching on foot. Most fittings of this sort are equipped with time delays so that they switch themselves off after a period of time.

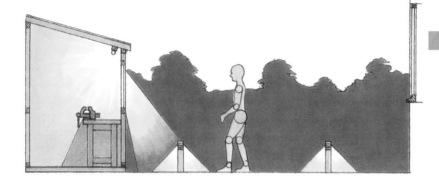

LIGHTING PATHWAYS

If an outbuilding is used regularly after dark, it may be convenient to be able to control its light from within the house. Similarly, if a shed is some distance from the house, it is a good idea to illuminate the path. In a garden small enough to have only one multi-purpose path, this could be part of the overall lighting scheme, but in a larger garden, it makes sense to install a dedicated circuit for access to any regularly used outbuilding. This may be a hard-wired installation, but a heat- or motion-triggered light would serve very well in this situation and could double as a part of the security system. Such luminaires are readily available from hardware stores and security-system retailers, and are simple to install.

FINDING YOUR WAY
Lighting the paths and driveways is probably the origin of all garden illumination and there is a good range of suitable luminaires available. To avoid light pollution, it is important that they are kept at a low level, and are shaded to minimize glare. Any steps, particularly if they are irregular, can be very dangerous if not illuminated.

145

LIGHTING FOR SECURITY

MANY PEOPLE TODAY ARE FEELING THE NEED FOR EXTERIOR LIGHTING FOR THE SAKE OF SECURITY, EVEN IF THEY HAVE NEVER ENTERTAINED ANY OTHER THOUGHTS OF LIGHTING THE GARDEN. SECURITY IS INDEED AN IMPORTANT PART OF A LIGHTING SCHEME, BUT IT SHOULD NOT, AND NEED NOT, COMPROMISE RECREATIONAL LIGHTING — THE LIGHTING FOR PLEASURE.

BORROWED LIGHTING

Light sources for exterior security lights may be all, or some, of those used for path or driveway lighting. In many ways this is a good and economical approach, but the lights may not be best positioned to answer both, quite different, sets of criteria, and it may not be practical to leave the path and driveway lighting on all night — it will certainly be expensive. If this is the chosen solution, there should be one group, or a series of groups, activated by motion- or heat-detecting switching and on separate circuits from the other garden lighting.

DARK-HOURS LIGHTING

If dark-hours (all-night) security lighting is required, bulkhead luminaires with compact fluorescents are ideal, since they use less power and have a long life span. Dark-hours lighting can be automated by installing light-detecting switches, such as those used to control the lighting in our streets and other public spaces. These switches are readily available from retailers. In this way, the security lighting comes on at dusk and goes off at dawn, even while the house is unoccupied.

CHOOSING FOR SECURITY
Outdoor security lighting is available in a huge variety of styles. A very exposed home (opposite) with vulnerable outbuildings would benefit from bulkhead-type lighting (top right), while the porches and entrances lend themselves to a more traditional-style of luminaire (centre and bottom right).

It is, however, worth noting that having lights on all night can play havoc with the natural cycles of local wildlife; with the recent increase in triggered security systems, this is now becoming a problem in both town and country. Although dark-hours lighting is an easy solution, with nature conservancy in mind, it may not be the best option.

TRIP SWITCHES

Installing a trip switch outside the house to control a light or group of lights on the inside may not be a familiar idea, but it can be most effective in raising doubt in the mind of a potential intruder. It would be possible to extend this system to include audio systems and televisions.

PLANNING FOR SECURITY

Security lighting can be as simple as a pair of coach lamps by the door, or a whole, sophisticated anti-intruder system. Large or small, it should be well-planned to maximize its use and minimize intrusions. Make a ground plan of your house and surrounds, marking approaches and walkways and identifying dark spots. Simply flooding the whole area will annoy both you and your neighbours, so the more careful your advanced planning the better (see also page 59).

USING ALTERNATIVES

Night-time security lighting is a compromise between the interests of security, the recreational lighting scheme and the environment. Neither of the latter benefit from a flood of light and, apart from the nuisance it can cause to neighbours, both human and animal, there is no certainty that it will provide any greater degree of security than a well thought-out and more subtle installation that incorporates a combination of the ideas in this chapter. A number of lower-powered lights placed in carefully selected positions, such as above doors and in exterior passageways, will do a more thorough job than one high-powered floodlight; they are more likely to deter intruders and will better satisfy the needs of your recreational scheme and of the environment.

GLOSSARY

A

Anti-UV
A treatment which filters out the ultraviolet end of the spectrum. This is often applied to windows in museums and art galleries to protect sensitive material, such as watercolour paintings.

B

Bayonet clip (BC) or bayonet base
A means of fixing a lamp into a lamp holder by means of two lugs. Known in the USA as a bayonet base.

Barn-doors
Flaps mounted in front of a spotlight to control the direction of its beam.

Beam
Light that is projected in a particular direction. The beam from a lamp is classified by its diameter, under 30° being a narrow beam and over 45° being a wide beam.

Blacklighters
A term used to describe lamps that emit ultraviolet light.

Bulb
The glass envelope that contains the filament, which together make a lamp.

Bulkhead luminaire
A wall-mounted luminaire protected by a metal grille. A maritime expression: the internal walls of ships, particularly those which divide them from side to side, are known as bulkheads.

Bus bar
A linear electric socket. Two continuous strips of copper wire, one positive and one negative, are mounted side-by-side, enabling power to be taken off at any point along their length. The most common form is in lighting track. The expression derives from the continuous bell push used in buses to enable passengers to signal the driver.

C

Candle holder
Any device which is intended to hold a candle or multiples of candles. Also the socket into which a candle is fixed.

Carbon filament
A very fine wire made from carbon, enclosed in a glass bulb containing an inert gas. An electric current passing through the filament causes it to become hot and emit light. The earliest practical 'electric light bulb', invented by Thomas Edison in 1879, was a carbon filament enclosed in a bulb containing a vacuum.

Carriage lamp
Originally a lamp fitted to a horse-drawn coach or carriage. Converted carriage lamps and reproductions later became popular for lighting either side of a house entrance. Nowadays any luminaire so placed, but which is not specifically a bulkhead, tends to be called a carriage lamp.

Ceiling rose
Originally the decorative plasterwork surrounding the point at which a luminaire was suspended from the ceiling. The term is now often applied to any plastic, electrical mounting box that holds a pendant luminaire.

Central pendant
The most common form of domestic lighting, this is a single or multiple lamp holder suspended from the ceiling at the centre of a room.

Chandelier
Originally a multiple candle holder, often festooned with cut crystal, intended to provide as much light as possible. Modern equivalents are multiple lamp holders often fitted with lamps shaped to imitate candles.

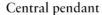

Chiaroscuro
The juxtaposition of extremes of light and shade to create dramatic effects.

Colour of light
The range of visible light, from red to blue, depending on the wavelength of that light. In printing terms, any colour can be made up from four base colours – cyan (blue), yellow, magenta and black. These, however, are pigment-based, not light-wave-based colours.

Compact biaxial
A form of fluorescent tube, in which two short tubes are mounted side-by-side. Also known as PL (an abbreviation for the Philips product).

Conduit
A tube, usually plastic, intended to carry electrical wiring and protect it from damage. In the USA the tube is usually steel. It can also be flexible, which is known as a Greenfield Connector.

Contact breaker
An automatic switch which cuts off the power in the event of a short circuit. See also ground-fault switch.

Cowl
The cover for a lamp which either creates a projector from an all-round-glow lamp or which hides a projector lamp from most angles, thereby reducing glare.

Crown-silvered lamp
A lamp in which the glass has a silver coating over its top, causing the light to be thrown backwards. They are manufactured to be used in conjunction with a parabolic reflector.

D

Dichroic reflector
A multi-faceted glass bowl coated in such a way as to project light forwards and conduct heat backwards.

Diffuse light
Light which is broadly scattered, creating perfectly even illumination over a relatively wide area. Diffused light tends to diminish shadow.

Dimmer
A mechanical or electronic means of controlling the output from a lamp or group of lamps.

Display lighting
Lighting which is intended to illuminate one or more items so that they may be seen to their best effect.

Down-lighting
A luminaire or number of luminaires intended to shine downwards only.

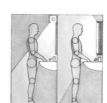

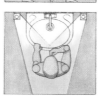

E

Efficiency
Energy efficiency, in lighting, is the ratio of light output to electricity consumption.

Edison screw (ES)
Designed by Thomas Edison, this is the second most common means of fixing a lamp into a lamp holder. Known in the USA as a screw base.

F

Filament
A fine piece of wire through which an electric current is passed, causing it to glow and give off light.

Filters
Sheets of glass or plastic which intercept light from a lamp. Commonly used to provide colour.

Flexible-arm light
A table lamp with a jointed arm which enables the lamp to be positioned in the most convenient place. Other forms use flexible tubing or similar devices.

Flood
A lamp whose beam exceeds 45° diameter, or a combination of lamp and cowl which achieves a similar result.

Fluorescence
The result of causing something to absorb invisible radiation and emit visible radiation. A phosphor coating on the inside of a tube or bulb is made to fluoresce, or glow, by ultraviolet radiation from mercury vapour.

Focal point
The point or points in a room or scene which are contrived to attract the eye.

Focus
The adjustment of eye or lens necessary to produce a clear image. Also, light which gives coherence to a group of separate objects, textures and surfaces that make up a room.

Flicker lamp
A form of lamp intended to imitate the natural light of a candle, which it singularly fails to do. The effect is interesting, however, and can be useful for special effects.

G

Gel
Heat-proof coloured-plastic sheeting placed over a light source in order to project colours, particularly in theatrical lighting.

General lighting service (GLS)
The most common lamps.

Ground fault switch
Safety device that cuts a circuit if it detects any leakage of current. Common in the USA. See also contact breaker.

Growth-enhancing tube
A fluorescent tube, often with pink-tinted glass, designed to emit wavelengths of light that promote plant growth.

I

Incandescence
The result of causing something to glow white-hot; the principle behind the electric light bulb, in which a carbon or tungsten wire (the filament) is caused to glow white-hot by passing an electric current through it.

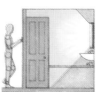

Incandescent mantle
A fine-silk net bag which is placed over the nozzle of a gas light. The gas flame heats the mantle, causing it to incandesce.

Infrared
The hot, red end of the light spectrum, invisible to the human eye.

Intensity
The level of output from a lamp, measured in lumens and lux.

K

Kerosene
The term for paraffin in North America, Australia and New Zealand.

L

Lamp
A light source comprising a filament encased in a bulb containing an inert gas.

Light
The medium of illumination emitted by a lamp.

Light strings
A length of wire to which lamp holders are fixed at pre-determined intervals. Also a length of plastic tube into which lamps are fixed at pre-determined intervals. The latter are often controlled electronically, enabling them to flash or light in pre-set sequences.

Lighting track
A linear power socket to which luminaires can be fixed at any point along its length. It comes in many forms, in both low and mains voltage.

Low voltage
Luminaires or lamps rated below the level of standard mains voltage are known as low-voltage, and require a transformer to step the power down to the appropriate level, usually 12V or 24V. Certain forms of transport, such as ships and cars, have complete low-voltage systems.

Lumen
The unit of light by which the output of a lamp is measured.

Luminaire
Any device designed or made to carry a lamp holder. As a rule it includes the lamp, lamp holder, shade, reflector and body but, at its most basic, a luminaire can be just a lamp and lamp holder.

Lux
The number of lumens per square metre.

M

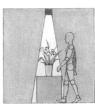

Mains voltage
A volt is the unit of electro-motive force by which domestic current is measured. Mains voltage is the level supplied by an electricity-generating company, and is usually 220V or 240V in the UK, and 110V in North America (doubled for large appliances).

Miniature spotlights
Specific types of small luminaire designed to carry a projector with a small cap. They are usually provided with a clamp which enables them to be positioned almost anywhere.

O

Opalescent shade
A shade made of semi-translucent glass, usually white.

P

Parabolic aluminized reflector (PAR)
A heavy glass projector lamp with an internal parabolic reflector, often with a lens moulded into the front of the bulb.

Parabolic reflector
A bowl made up as a three-dimensional parabola, with a reflective internal surface. Used in conjunction with a crown-silvered lamp, it concentrates the light and projects it forward in a tightly controlled beam.

Paraffin
Inflammable oil or wax produced by distillation from petroleum or shale and used as a fuel, illuminant or lubricant.

Path-lighter
A luminaire specifically

designed to illuminate a path, usually with a wide, flat shade that prevents any light being projected upwards.

Pearl lamp
A lamp made with a semi-translucent bulb that diffuses the light.

Pigment
A natural or synthetic chemical compound used as colouring matter in paint or dye.

Pressure lamp
A portable luminaire with a reservoir of liquid fuel, usually paraffin, which turns to gas when heated under pressure. The pressure forces the gas through a nozzle, where it is ignited and heats a cotton mantle, causing it to incandesce and produce a strong, white light.

Projector
A lamp designed to throw its light forwards in a controlled beam. Also an apparatus for projecting rays of light or projecting an image onto a screen or wall.

R

Rated average life (RAL)
The number of hours that 50 per cent of lamps of any given type survive being on continuously.

Rise-and-fall luminaire
A pendant luminaire designed to be moved up or down to a convenient level. The idea originated in the era of gas lighting when it was necessary to lower a luminaire in order to light the gas.

Rushlight
The pith of a rush or reed soaked in fuel and ignited.

S

Shade
A device which shields light from direct view. Also the area of relative darkness created.

Shielded down-lighter
A luminaire in which the lamp is recessed into a tube, thereby concealing the light source.

Soft-tone
A bulb dyed in one of a range of pastel colours.

Spectrum
The colour range of visible light observable in a rainbow or when a beam is split with a prism.

Spot
A beam of light with a diameter of less than 35°.

Standard lamp
A tall, free-standing luminaire consisting of a lamp holder with a decorative body.

Stepped-down power
Low-voltage power achieved by passing mains voltage through a transformer.

T

Table lamp
A short, free-standing luminaire consisting of a lamp holder with a decorative body.

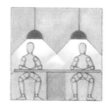

Task lighting
Lighting which is designed to illuminate a specific task or activity.

Toggle switch
A press switch which remains on until pressed again.

Tone
The quality of emitted light.

Toroidal transformer
A compact transformer made in the form of a torus, or semicircular ring. This form allows it to be fitted into the base of a luminaire.

Torpedo switch
A switch mounted at any point along a length of flexible electric cable.

Track lighting
See lighting track.

Tungsten-filament
A very fine wire made from tungsten. An electrical current passing through a tungsten filament enclosed in a glass bulb containing a mixture of argon and nitrogen, causes the wire to become white-hot and give off light.

Tungsten-halogen
A lamp made of fused-quartz glass filled with halogen and argon, which achieves greater light output for less energy than a standard tungsten-filament lamp.

U

Ultraviolet (UV)
Light emitted at the blue extreme of the visible spectrum.

Up-lighting
A luminaire or number of luminaires intended to shine upwards only.

W

Wall socket
A power outlet mounted into or onto the surface of a wall.

Wall-mounted up-lighter
A luminaire which has a shade designed to be fixed to a vertical surface and project the light upwards only.

Wall washer
A luminaire designed to illuminate flat vertical surfaces only.

Wattage
The output rating of a lamp.

Wick
An absorbent material, usually a cord or tape, soaked in fuel and ignited.

INDEX

Page numbers in *italic* refer to
illustrations and captions

PHOTOGRAPHS

British Home Stores/Chris Beckett 14 (all left apart from Tiffany/Christopher Wray second from bottom right), 58 (right), 59 (above and below), 63 (below), 106 (left and right), 146 (below);

Christopher Wray 14 (left), 39, 41, 42, 46 (above), 47 (left and right), 48 (left and right), 49 (left), 50 (right), 51, 52 (left), 53(left), 55 (right above and below), 58 (left), 61, 105 (above), 110;

Davey & Company 146 (above), 147;

Elizabeth Whiting Associates 2, 5, 10, 12, 13, 14 (right above & below), 15, 16, 19, 21 (left), 22, 23, 24 (above left, right and below), 25, 26-7, 27, 28, 29, 30 (above and below), 31 (above and below), 32, 34, 36, 38 (left and right), 46 (left), 54, 55 (left), 56, 64, 66 (above and below), 67 (above, below and right), 68, 69 (above and below), 70, 71, 73, 74 (above and below), 75, 76, 77 (above and below), 78, 79 (above and below), 80, 81 (above and below), 82, 83, 84 (above left, right and below), 85, 86, 88 (above left, right and below), 89, 90, 91, 92, 95 (all), 96, 97, 99, 100 (all), 101, 102, 103, 104 (all), 105 (below), 107 (above and below), 108, 109 (left and right), 111 (left and right), 112, 114, 115, 116 (left and right), 117, 118, 120, 121, 124, 126 (above), 128, 129, 130 (above and below), 131, 132, 133, 134 (left above and below), 136, 137, 139 (right), 140, 141, 142, 143 (left and right), 146 (middle), 147 (right);

GE Lighting 45, 46 (below), 49 (right), 50 (above), 52 (right), 53 (left);

Lightbox 35;

Oase 125,134 (right above and below), 135 (all);

Optelma 18, 20, 21 (right), 62, 122 (above and below), 123, 127 (left and right), 144, 145 (left and right);

Science Photo Library 6, 33;

Stapeley Water Gardens 126 (right above and below);

Stephen Wynne 63 (above), 138, 139 (left), 160;

Sylvania 49 (middle), 50 (below);

Visual Arts Library 9 (left and right).